D0115043

The 250 Job Interview Questions

You'll Most Likely Be Asked ...
and the answers that will get you hired!

PETER VERUKI

Aadamsmedia
Avon, Massachusetts

Copyright © 2010, 1999 by F+W Media, Inc.
All rights reserved. This book, or parts thereof, may not be reproduced in any
form without permission from the publisher; exceptions are made for brief
excerpts used in published reviews.

Published by Adams Business, an imprint of Adams Media,
a division of F+W Media, Inc.
57 Littlefield Street, Avon, MA 02322. U.S.A.
www.adamsmedia.com

ISBN 10: 1-58062-117-1
ISBN 13: 978-1-58062-117-5

Printed in the United States of America.

10 9 8 7 6 5 4 3 2 1

Library of Congress Cataloging-in-Publication Data
is available from the publisher.

This publication is designed to provide accurate and authoritative information
with regard to the subject matter covered. It is sold with the understanding
that the publisher is not engaged in rendering legal, accounting, or other professional advice. If legal advice or other expert assistance is required, the services of a competent professional person should be sought.
—From a *Declaration of Principles* jointly adopted by a Committee of the
American Bar Association and a Committee of Publishers and Associations

Many of the designations used by manufacturers and sellers to distinguish
their products are claimed as trademarks. Where those designations appear in
this book and Adams Media was aware of a trademark claim, the designations
have been printed with initial capital letters.

This book is available at quantity discounts for bulk purchases.
For information, call 1-800-289-0963.

CONTENTS

Okay, so you've scheduled a job interview—or maybe even a few. Now what? This chapter will show you six key ways to turn your job interviews into job offers, including how to develop your personal themes for the interview and how to research potential employers.

Here you'll find all the tips you need for setting the right tone. Topics include dressing for success, what to bring with you, the importance of body language, overcoming nervousness, and presenting a professional image.

This chapter will show you how to navigate an interview conversation. It presents the differences between first and second interviews and the strategies you should employ. You'll also find typical questions that you can ask them.

This chapter presents two hundred of the most common interview questions you must be prepared to answer. The questions are arranged in an order consistent with the themes described in Chapter 1. Most interviews are based on these questions, or variations of the ones that appear here and in Chapter 5.

Here you'll learn how to handle killer interview questions with finesse, including specific questions for first-time job seekers, experienced professionals, career changers, and other special groups. There's also a special section on handling illegal interview questions.

PART 3

You flew through your interview without problems. Now what? This chapter will show you how to follow-up on first interviews with sections on writing a follow-up e-mail, handling rejection, and moving on to the next step.

Here you'll learn about the important factors to consider when weighing an offer, including salary, benefits, work environment, and more. This chapter also includes expert negotiating techniques to help you get what you want.

ACKNOWLEDGMENTS

Thanks to the following people whose generous time and expertise made this book possible:

Virginia Alonzo, Javier Amador-Peña, Rebecca Jesperson Anthony, Linda Armstrong, Linda Arslanian, MS, PT, Jennifer Barr, Elise Bauman, Susan Beale, Edward Beaudoin, Julianne Bennett, Jeff Benson, Bill Brands, Russell Brothers, Rob Bunnell, Michael J. Carriero, Christopher Ciaschini, Elizabeth Clarke, Nicole Coady, Marisa Cohen, Andrew J. Conn, Susan Crawford, Catherine Crowder, Bob Davis, Dental Fill-Ins, Laura DiBenedetti, John J. Diggins, Richard Dreier, James B. Earley, Lisa Edenton, Katy Edmonson, Jeff Eisnaugle, Anny Ellis, Glen Fassinger, Joanne Franco, Jill Gabbe, Jan Gentry, Clifton Gerring, Dov Goldman, Al Golub, Jeffrey M. Graeber, Jim Grobman, Ron Grover, Steve Grune, Bob Hale, Pete Harper, Gary Hayden, Margot T. Healy, RD, Catherine A. Hegan, Catherine Holsen, Denise Humphrey, Beryl Israel, Wayne Jackson, Michelle Johnson, Chuck Kelly, Keith Kleinsmith, J. Patrick Knuff, Linda Kosarin, Jennifer Kove, Rowena R. Krum, Heather Kuty, David E. Lambert, Jr., Ann C. Lee, Howard Levinson, CPP, Pam Liflander, Mark A. Linnus, Andrew Lobo, Michael G. McArdle, Mark McAuley, John McCauley, Nancy McGovern, Terence McGovern, MSW, LICSW, Jim Mellarkey, Bruce Menin, Arnold Most, Jennifer Most, Karen M. Nichols, Elizabeth O'Brien, Carrie Oliver, Richard Oliver, Susan Oliver,

Guy Pacitti, Stefan Pagacik, Thomas V. Patton, Pam Perry, Joe Petrie, Jeff Phillips, Rosalie Prosser, Jan Quiram, Rodney Ramsey, Gigi Ranno, Andy Richardson, Gary P. Richardson, Alan Ritchie, Kent Rodgers, Gerald Roe, Bob Rogers, Thomas J. Rusin, David Ryback, Jeremy M. Sherber, Donna Shervanian, Aryana Soebagjo, Judy Spinella, John Stagliano, Joseph Steur, Deborah Story, Allan Tatel, Bob Teague, Jill Todd, Nancy True, Catherine Tuttle, K. A. Vlahos, Mark Waldstein, David Williams, Ron Wilson, Frank Winslow, David S. Wolff, Bill York, Diane V. Yurkewicz, Reeve Zimmerman, Michael Zitomer, and Frank J. Zych, Jr.

INTRODUCTION

Jobs are won and lost in the interview.

After all, this is the employer's best chance to evaluate what you'll bring to the job, how you'll fit in with the team, and what role you can play in the future of the company. Over the years, employers and Human Rights professionals have evolved a battery of questions that are designed to bring out the most revealing answers.

Behind all of these questions is the fact that the hiring manager has a *problem*. This, after all, is why he or she is considering hiring you. The manager wants to know how you'll solve that problem. Figure out what the problem is and how you can provide a solution to it, and the job is yours.

Especially when times are tough and jobs are few and far between, the interview process scares many people. Faced with a hiring manager's questions, they often freeze up or give minimal responses. That's where this book comes in.

Whether you're recently laid off, a job-changer, a recent graduate, or someone re-entering the workforce, in these pages you'll find the 250 most commonly asked interview questions. There are many more you'll be asked that are specific to the company and industry for which you're interviewing. But these are the essential ones.

This is not to say you should memorize all the responses listed in this book and reel them off to the interviewer. Rather, the idea is for you to familiarize yourself with the commonly asked questions and prepare your answers in advance so you feel more prepared and confident when sitting across the desk from the hiring manager or HR manager. Use the responses you find here to shape your own answers—answers that will demonstrate what a valuable asset you'll be to the company. During the interview, if you listen carefully to the questions you're being asked—and listening is one of the most valuable of all interview skills—you can learn what qualities the company values. With that information, you can tailor your answers in real-time to make the best possible impression.

Inside, you'll also find advice on how to prepare for the interview, research potential employers, and develop your own themes for the interview. There's a section that brings to light certain questions that are illegal for employers to bring up; but you may, nonetheless, be asked to answer them. It's important to be prepared for questions like this and know how to respond without dooming your chances of landing the job. Finally, you'll get tips on negotiating the final offer so you can secure the job you *really* want.

Many things have changed in the workplace over the years as the economy has risen and fallen and the job market has tightened and eased. But the basics of how to interview well remain the same:

1. Make an impression so you stand out from the crowd.
2. Be responsive and sincere in your answers.
3. Radiate professionalism.
4. Show how you can contribute positively to the company and to the team.

In today's job market, these things are more important than ever. So read through the questions in this book, do your homework, take a deep breath, and walk into the interview with your head held high. You've got a great career ahead of you!

PART 1

Before the Job Interview

Chapter **1**

PREPARING FOR THE INTERVIEW

Too many job seekers jump right into a full-scale job search without much advance preparation other than putting together a resume. A serious mistake! Although your resume may get you job interviews, to win job offers, you must prepare yourself further. It's vitally important to distinguish yourself in some positive way from other candidates vying for the same position. One way of accomplishing this is by developing several themes that you continually refer to throughout the job interview. This enables you to emphasize your strongest points and ensures that you'll leave a positive impression in the recruiter's mind.

Developing Your Personal Themes for the Job Interview

There are twelve types of information recruiters seek in a typical job interview. Knowing what these points are, and being able to discuss readily how each point relates to you, will make you better prepared and more in control of the interviewing process. Think of your twelve themes as sales messages. Each is designed to showcase your best skills and qualifications. Together, they make up a twelve-point strategy that will enable you to sell your qualifications in virtually any interview situation.

Read through the following twelve topics. Develop a personalized approach to each and practice talking about it. Think of specific examples in your background that correspond to each topic. You can't possibly be prepared for every situation, but once you've developed your twelve key messages, you'll be able to apply them to almost any interview question you face.

Next, turn to Chapter 4 to review common interview questions relating to each of the twelve themes. Try to answer each question aloud, incorporating the themes you've developed. Then evaluate your progress. You may discover that you need more practice in order to become comfortable discussing the topics in a clear and concise manner. Nothing that you say for the first time will come out the way you like. Practice aloud delivering your twelve key messages until the words come easily in an organized yet comfortable, conversational way.

1. Passion for the Business

Ask yourself, "Why am I interested in working in this field in this industry?" Do you feel a passion for the business? If so, why? Give specific examples of the things that excite you. These could be anything from enjoying the challenge of meeting increasingly higher sales goals, to a sense of satisfaction derived from developing a product from the creation stage to final production. Offer personal experience where possible.

2. Motivation and Purpose

Interviewers will want to know why you want to work for their particular company. Ask yourself, "Why do I want this interview?" Don't simply repeat your resume and employment history. What's the most compelling case you can make to prove your interest? Have you used the company's products or talked to its customers or competitors? (Refer to the section that follows, "Researching Potential Employers," to learn how you can locate this kind of information about companies you're interested in.)

3. Skills and Experience

Consider your key skills and how you'll use them in this job. Avoid clichés and generalities; instead, offer specific evidence. Think about your weaknesses and how you can minimize and balance them with your strengths. Try to describe yourself as objectively as possible. Avoid sounding arrogant or defensive.

4. Diligence and Professionalism

Describe your professional character, including thoroughness, diligence, and accountability. Give proof that you persevere to see important projects through, and that you achieve desired results. Demonstrate how you gather resources, how you predict obstacles, and how you manage stress.

5. Creativity and Leadership

Offer proof of your effectiveness, including creativity, initiative, resourcefulness, and leadership. What examples can you provide for each? Focus on how you overcome problems, how you take advantage of opportunities that might otherwise be overlooked, and how you rally the support of others to accomplish goals.

6. Compatibility with the Job

Discuss your specific qualifications for the job. How well do they fit the requirements of the position? Your answer should describe both positive and negative aspects of recent jobs, without dwelling on the negatives. Conclude by focusing on what you're seeking in your next job. Keep in mind that your response should match closely the position you're applying for.

7. Personality and Cultural Compatibility

Consider your personality on the job. How do you fit in with other types of personalities? What types of people would enjoy working with you for hours at a time? How would the company's customers or clients react to you? Your goal is to develop responses that make the interviewer feel confident there won't be any surprises about your personality on the job.

8. Management Style and Interpersonal Skills

Talk about the management style and the interpersonal skills you use with peer groups and leaders. Focus on how you work rather than on what type of work you do well. What kind of boss, colleague, and employee will you be? Give personal or popular examples of leaders you believe are effective. Why are those people able to accomplish so much?

9. Problem-Solving Ability

Offer proof, with examples, of your problem-solving ability. How have you resolved difficult issues in the past? Are you practical in how you apply technical skills? Are you realistic? Focus on real issues, on logical value-added solutions, on practical outcomes of your work, and on realistic measures of judging these outcomes.

10. Accomplishments

Think about your initiative and accomplishments. Offer examples in which you've delivered more than what was expected. Don't give long descriptions of situations; instead, focus your answer on the action you took and the positive results you obtained. If you were hired, what situations would you handle especially well? What can you contribute to the organization?

11. Career Aspirations

Tailor your aspirations to the realities of this particular job and its career path. Avoid listing job titles or offering unrealistic performance deadlines. Instead, reiterate the skills and strengths you want to develop further. Do you want cross-functional experience, a larger budget, or more supervisory responsibility? Why would you be effective with that additional experience?

12. Personal Interests and Hobbies

Do you have a balanced lifestyle? Is your personality reflected in the type of job you choose as well as in the outside activities you pursue? Are your personal and career interests compatible? The interviewer will also be interested in your community involvement. How commendably would you reflect the company's image?

After you feel comfortable with your twelve sales messages, develop them in a brief summary. This is a useful tool that you can use effectively at the end of the interview, when the interviewer says something like "Is there anything else you'd like to tell me?" Never let an interview end without summarizing your twelve key messages.

The Sixty-Second Pitch

Another good preparation technique is the sixty-second pitch. Approximately one week after you've sent your resume to a key decision maker, you should follow up with a phone call. Don't simply ask if your resume has been received—this can be frustrating to employers who are inundated with hundreds of resumes. A better approach is to state that you've sent your resume and explain, in sixty seconds or less, why you think you're the best candidate for the position. Your sixty-second pitch should be a clear and concise summary of yourself, including three important elements:

- What kind of work you do (or want to do)
- What your strongest skills and accomplishments are
- What kind of position you're seeking

If you're invited to an interview after you've pitched yourself to the hiring manager, great! If not, don't let it end there! Ask if there are any particular qualifications that he or she is looking for in a candidate. Is there anything else you can do or any additional information that you can send (writing samples, clippings, or portfolio) to help the hiring manager make a decision? Even if the person says no, that your resume is sufficient, he or she may be impressed by your interest and enthusiasm.

If you haven't already done so, specifically ask the employer if he or she would have a few minutes to meet with you. If that doesn't work, ask if that person knows anyone who might be interested in speaking to someone with your qualifications. If you're unable to arrange an interview or to get a referral, ask the employer if he or she would mind if you called back in a month or so. The goal is to get a positive response from the phone call—whether it's an interview or simply a scrap of job-hunting advice. Don't give up too easily, but be professional and courteous at all times.

Researching Potential Employers

There are two good reasons why you should set aside some time early in your job search to research companies in your field of interest. First, it's a great way to locate potential employers. Second, it's an effective way to learn more about particular companies you're considering working for.

Researching potential employers can be time-consuming, but it's well worth the effort. To use your time effectively, however, you should divide your research into two distinct phases. The first phase should involve gathering only basic information about many different companies, including:

- Company name, address, phone and fax numbers
- Names and job titles of key contacts
- Whether the company is privately or publicly held
- Products and/or services
- Year of incorporation
- Number of employees

The second phase of research begins as you start to schedule job interviews. This involves gathering more detailed information about each company you're interviewing with. Your goal is to be able to walk into an interview knowing the organization inside and out. You need to know the company's products, types of customers, subsidiaries, parent company, principal locations, rank in the industry, sales and profit trends, type of ownership, size, current plans, principal competitors and their relative performance, and much more. Incorporating this knowledge into your discussions is certain to impress the toughest of interviewers and will distinguish you from the competition. The more time you spend on this phase, the better prepared you'll be. Even if you feel extremely pressed for time, you should set aside at least twelve hours for preinterview research.

Where To Look

To find the information you need, you'll have to dig into every resource you can find. Libraries are a fantastic source of both publicized and hidden job opportunities. Most have a vast array of resources, including major newspapers like the *New York Times* and the *Wall Street Journal* and trade journals like *Advertising Age* and *Publishers Weekly*. To identify publications in your field of interest, consult the *Encyclopedia of Business Information Sources* or Predicasts *F&S Index*.

There are a number of other resources you can use to find listings of companies, most of which can also be found at your local library. Ask the reference librarian to help you locate the many directories that list basic information about companies in your field of interest. Be sure not to overlook these great tools:

> Dun and Bradstreet's *Million Dollar Directory*, in print and online, lists approximately 160,000 companies that are both publicly and privately held and is updated annually. *www.dnlearn.com*

> *Standard & Poor's Register of Corporations* lists fewer companies than the Million Dollar Directory (about 45,000) but provides valuable biographical information on thousands of company officials.

Corporate Technology Directory (Corporate Technology Information Services) focuses on the products of approximately 35,000 companies. This is a great resource for job seekers interested in high-tech industries, including computers, biotechnology, environmental engineering, chemical and pharmaceutical, and transportation. *www.corptech.com*

Personnel Executives Contactbook (Gale Research) lists key personnel and other contacts at 30,000 publicly and privately held companies and government agencies.

The National JobBank (Adams Media Corporation) lists key contacts at over 21,000 small and large American companies. It includes information on common positions filled and educational backgrounds desired and is updated annually.

Directory of Human Resources Executives (Hunt–Scanlon) names human-resource executives and provides information on number of employees and area of specialization of 5,000 public and private companies.

Directory of Corporate Affiliations (National Register) is one of the few places where you can find information on a company's divisions and subsidiaries. This book lists information on approximately 4,000 parent companies.

Also, don't overlook the countless industry-specific directories that are available, such as *The JobBank Guide to Computer & High-Tech Companies, The JobBank Guide to Health Care Companies, Dunn's Directory of Service Companies, Martindale-Hubbell Law Directory,* and *Standard Directory of Advertisers.* These are terrific places to find potential employers and often include information on professional associations and industry trends.

All these resources and more can be accessed online. A few clicks of your mouse can find you thousands of listings for companies. Sites such as *www.hoovers.com*, *www.corptech.com*, and *www.business.com* are a good starting place for your research. Virtually all the newspapers and magazines mentioned earlier have online searchable versions available to you for free or for a modest fee. As well, many company websites post key information.

After perusing these sites, call the investor-relations departments of companies you're interested in and request a hardcopy of their annual report. (This approach will generally work only with larger companies.) Call the sales office or PR office of the parent company to get a copy of any literature distributed to consumers, including product literature, recent press releases, or even annual reports (for public companies). If the company is public, call a stockbroker and ask for additional information to supplement what's already in your file. If the firm has a human-resources department, ask for a recruitment package or any other information available to job seekers. If you're interested in a smaller company that doesn't have a human-resources department or publish annual reports, don't panic! Most companies have brochures or catalogs of their products or services that they'll send to you upon request. If possible, speak to someone at the firm before the interview. If you can't do this, speak to someone at a competing firm. The more time you spend, the better.

Use all of your research to develop educated, informed opinions. You'll be better prepared to exchange ideas, create interesting conversation, and make a positive impression on the interviewer.

The Informational Interview

Particularly if you're an entry-level job seeker or a career changer, you should consider conducting at least one informational interview.

An informational interview is simply a meeting that you arrange to talk to someone in a field, industry, or company that interests you. With the help of this kind of interview, you can prepare for a real job interview in several ways, including:

- Examining your compatibility with the company by comparing the realities of the field (skills required, working conditions, schedules, and common traits of people you meet) to your own personal interests
- Finding out how people in a particular business, industry, or job view their roles and the growth opportunities in their businesses
- Conducting primary research on companies and industries
- Gaining insight into the kinds of topics your potential interviewers will be concerned about and the methods for interviewing
- Getting feedback on your relative strengths and weaknesses as a potential job candidate
- Becoming comfortable talking to people in the industry and learning the industry jargon
- Building your network, which can lead to further valuable information and opportunities

To set up an informational appointment, request a meeting with someone who has at least several years' experience working in your field of interest. Your goal is to learn how that person got into the business, what he or she likes about it, and what kind of advice someone with experience might pass on to someone who's interested in entering the field.

Tell your contact right away that you'd like to learn more about the industry or company, and that you'll be the one asking all the questions. Most people won't feel threatened (especially if you assure them you're not asking them for a job) and will usually be inclined to help you.

If you tell a contact that all you want is advice, though, make sure you mean it. Never approach an informational interview as though it were a job interview—just stick to gathering information and leads and see what happens. Also, unless specifically requested to do so, sending your resume to someone you'd like to meet for an informational interview will probably give the wrong impression.

Conducting Informational Interviews

Now that you've scheduled an informational interview, make sure you're prepared to take the lead. After all, you're the one doing the interviewing—not vice versa. Prepare a list of ten to twenty questions, such as:

- How did you get started in this business?
- What experience helped you to be prepared and qualified for this job? (How did you get to this point in your career?)
- What do you believe is the ideal education and background?
- What are your primary responsibilities in your current job?
- What do you like most about your job, your company, and your industry?
- What do you dislike most about them?
- What's been your greatest challenge?
- If you could work with anybody in this field, whom would you want to work with?
- Five years out, what are your career goals?
- What are typical career path options from here?
- If you could change something about your career path, what would you change?
- What are the most valuable skills to have in this field?
- What specific experiences helped you build these skills?
- What opportunities do you see in this business?
- Why did you want this job?

- What would you say are the current career opportunities for someone with my qualifications in the industry?
- If you were in the job market tomorrow, how would you get started? What would you do?
- What are the basic requirements for an entry-level position in the industry?
- What do you consider a must-read list in your field?
- Where do you see the industry heading in the near future?
- Is there a trade association that might aid me in my job search?
- What things impress you when you interview candidates for positions in this field?
- What are turnoffs when you interview candidates?
- What critical questions should I expect to be asked in a job interview?
- What advice would you give to someone looking for a job in the industry?
- Is there anything else I should know about the industry?
- Do you know of anyone who might be looking for someone with my qualifications?
- Is there anything you think I should've brought up (but didn't) that should be a consideration?

Always end by thanking the person and promising to follow up on any important leads he or she has provided and to let the person know how things turn out. You should also send a thank-you note within one or two days of the informational interview.

Follow up periodically with everyone in your network—even after you get a job. Once you develop a network, it's important not to lose those contacts. You want to translate your informational network into a support network and maintain it throughout your career.

Preparing for Telephone Interviews

Telephone screening interviews are becoming more commonplace because companies want to reduce their hiring costs by avoiding travel at screening stages in interviews. Using phone interviews, recruiters can quickly weed out most candidates and decide on the best candidates to pursue—that is, to invite for a face-to-face interview. This is when developing a sixty-second pitch can also come in handy.

Here's why planning for a telephone interview is so important: unlike a planned first interview, for which you have done all the preparation already discussed, a telephone interview can come at any time and from any company. Also, once you begin to network, a phone interview may result when all you expected was possible leads. Sometimes recruiters will call to schedule an interview at a later time, but more often they'll call hoping to interview you on the spot.

Here are some general tips for handling a phone interview:

- If you feel unprepared or uncomfortable with your phone skills, practice with a friend. Role-play and ask a friend to question you over the phone. Also, you can make good use of your answering machine, here; call when you're away from home and leave yourself a message emphasizing one of your themes. When you get home, listen to how you sound; listen to your voice pattern (enthusiasm, highs/lows, pauses, and so on). Also listen to the content—was your message clear and direct? Keep practicing until you're comfortable with the results.
- Always be prepared, with your twelve themes ready to go. The basic guidelines of a screening interview apply here as well.
- Keep a copy of your resume by the phone, along with a list of key words representing the themes you think are relevant to the industry or job category you're pursuing.

- You can't count on clues from an interviewer's body language, eye contact, or other such signs. You'll have to pay close attention, instead, to their voice pattern, and you must use your own voice—simple, direct, enthusiastic responses—to keep the conversation interesting and easy to follow.
- Listen very carefully and maintain your highest level of concentration. Have a phone set up where you can sit more or less as you'd sit for an interview. Keep a pen and some paper near the phone, along with your resume and notes. Take very careful notes about what you're asked and what seemed most critical to the recruiter. (This information will help you follow up later with a letter.)
- Avoid long pauses; provide quick summaries of your key themes or points with clear examples of how you've made positive contributions where you've been and how you could contribute to this company.
- Make sure you get the name (spelled correctly), number, and address of the person who called.
- Reaffirm your interest—if you're interested after this first round. Find out what happens next and what you can do to make yourself competitive. Follow up with a thank-you note, just as you would for a screening interview. Your goal is to get face-to-face in the next round.

Collecting References

At some point before you start interviewing, you'll need to prepare a list of three to five references. Unless you're new to the workforce, at least two of these should be professional references from previous employers or close business associates. Other potential sources of references include teachers, professors, volunteer committee heads, and friends who are well respected in business circles. Don't list family members as references.

Be sure to ask people for their permission before you cite them as references. If they agree, be sure you have their job title, the name of the company where they work, and their work address and phone number. Then prepare a neat, typed list of your reference contacts with your name at the top of the page. You should make several copies and have them on hand during your job interviews. Don't make the mistake of listing your references on your resume, as this is commonly considered inappropriate and unprofessional.

Don't forget to send each of your references a thank-you e-mail when your job search is over. Proper etiquette aside, this practice will help keep your contacts current. You never know when you might need their help again sometime down the road.

Chapter **2**

SETTING THE RIGHT TONE

You're on your way to a job interview.

By now, you've probably spent a great deal of time preparing. However, you must not let your practice and preparation become a disadvantage. Once the interview begins, you must focus on interacting effectively with the interviewer—as opposed to trying to recall precisely the responses you practiced earlier. If you've prepared adequately for the interview, your conduct and responses should effortlessly convey to the interviewer the image you want to project.

It's important for you to know that the interviewer's decision about whether or not you'll be invited back for an additional interview will probably be influenced by your attitude and personality as much as by your qualifications. So although preparation is important, your performance during an interview can make an even greater difference. Generally, you should try to stress the following qualities in your choice of words, your tone of voice, and your body language:

- Capability
- Confidence
- Dependability

- Easygoing manner
- Enthusiasm
- Flexibility
- Resourcefulness
- Strong work ethic

A word of caution: Don't concentrate too much on trying to project the perfect image. Just try to relax, visualize yourself as smooth and confident, and you'll almost certainly do well.

Dressing for Success

How important is proper dress for a job interview? Although the final selection of a job candidate will rarely be determined by dress, first-round candidates are often eliminated because they've dressed inappropriately. This is not to say you should invest in a new wardrobe; just be sure that you're able to put together an adequate interview outfit. A good rule of thumb is to dress for a position just above the one you're applying for.

Men should wear a clean, conservative, two-piece suit; a white shirt; and a silk tie. Lace-up wing tips are your best bet for shoes. This is the basic corporate wardrobe; however, in some industries, a quality jacket, pants, shirt, and tie are fine. But if you're not sure what dress is appropriate at a certain firm, play it safe and opt for a two-piece suit. A man should always wear a jacket and tie to an interview—even if everyone else in the office is in shirtsleeves. Dressing this way shows that you're taking the interview seriously and treating the company with respect.

For women, a professional-looking dress or suit with low-heeled shoes makes the best impression. In more conservative industries, like law or banking, a suit's probably your best choice. However, some hiring managers in creative industries, like advertising or publishing, look for a more informal, stylish look that reflects the applicant's individuality. Use your best judgment and wear whatever is both professional and comfortable for you. However, be sure to avoid excess jewelry or makeup.

Impeccable personal grooming is even more important than finding the perfect outfit. Be sure that your clothes are clean, pressed, and well fitting, and that your shoes are polished. Hair should be neat and businesslike, and your nails should be clean and trimmed. Both men and women are advised to skip the cologne or perfume—you never know if the person interviewing you will be violently allergic to the cologne you're wearing.

Timing Is Everything

Although it may seem hard to believe, many job seekers arrive late for interviews. This is easy enough to do—you might simply take a little unplanned extra time to prepare for your interview or underestimate how long it will take to get to the interview location. Don't let yourself make this fatal mistake!

Allow plenty of time to get ready for, and to travel to, your job interview. You shouldn't arrive at the interviewer's office more than ten minutes in advance. However, if you're driving across town, allowing yourself an extra ten minutes probably isn't enough. Try to get to the location at least thirty minutes early; you can then spend twenty minutes in a nearby coffee shop or take a walk around the building. Interviews are important enough to build in a little extra time. Here's another tip: If you've never been to the interview location, visit it the day before so you know exactly how to get there, how to access the building, and where to park.

Sometimes the interviewer will be running behind schedule. Don't be upset: be sympathetic. Interviewers are often pressured to see a lot of candidates and to fill a demanding position quickly. So be sure to come to your interview with good reading material to keep yourself occupied and relaxed.

What to Have on Hand

A briefcase or leather-bound folder, if you have one, will help complete the professional, polished look you want to achieve. Women should avoid carrying a purse if they plan on carrying a briefcase—it may detract from a professional image. And don't forget to wear a watch!

Before leaving for the interview, be sure that you have good directions and the phone numbers and names of the people you'll be meeting with. You should also bring the following items with you to the interview:

- Several unfolded copies of your resume and cover letter
- A notepad and pen (for taking notes during the interview)
- A list of professional references
- Examples of your work, such as writing samples or clippings (taking care that these don't breach the confidentiality of previous employers)

Body Language

The first minutes of the interview are the most important. A recruiter begins sizing up your potential the instant you walk into the room. If you make a bad impression from the start, you may be ruled out immediately, and the interviewer may pay little attention to your performance during the rest of the interview. An excellent initial impression, on the other hand, will put a favorable glow on everything else you say during the rest of the interview—and could well encourage the recruiter to ask less demanding questions.

How can you ensure that you make a terrific first impression? The easiest answer is to be sure you're dressed well. When the recruiter meets you, he or she will notice your clothes and grooming first. Nothing other than impeccable grooming is acceptable. Your attire must be professional and squeaky clean.

Your body language will also speak volumes, even before you and the interviewer exchange a word. Any recruiter will unconsciously pick up on and react to the subtle signals of body language. Here are some important things to think about:

- Do you smile when you meet?
- Do you make just enough eye contact without staring at the recruiter?
- Do you walk into the office with a self-assured and confident stride?
- Do you shake hands firmly?
- Are your briefcase, notepad, and coat in your left hand, or do you have to juggle them around in order to shake hands?
- Do your eyes travel naturally to and from the recruiter's face as you begin to talk?
- Do you remember the recruiter's name and pronounce it with confidence?
- Do you make small talk easily, or do you act formal and reserved, as though under attack?

It's human nature to judge people by that first impression, so make sure yours is a good one. But most of all, try to be yourself.

Overcoming Nervousness

As if formulating solid answers to interview questions isn't tough enough, you'll also have to overcome a quite natural, inevitable nervousness. Most employers won't think less of a job candidate for a bit of nervous behavior—but they will pay close attention to how you hold up under pressure. Displaying excessive nervousness can easily eliminate you from further consideration.

One good way to overcome preinterview jitters is to exercise positive thinking. If you're feeling nervous about an upcoming interview, imagine in detail what the experience will be like: Think of what you'll say, the questions you'll be asked, and how you'll answer them. Picture yourself responding calmly, effectively, and in a controlled manner. This type of mental rehearsing won't guarantee success, but it should help you feel more optimistic and self-confident, which will undoubtedly enhance your final presentation.

Above all, you should practice interviewing as much as you can. You'll become more confident and your answers will become more polished with each interview you have.

Chapter 3

INTERVIEW STRATEGIES

Navigating the Dynamics of Interview Conversation

All your preparation should be evident when the conversation gets going. Make sure your tone remains conversational; don't let the interview turn into an interrogation. Start by thanking the interviewer for the opportunity to talk with him or her and explain up front why you're interested in the position. Be ready to answer and to ask questions, including occasionally asking the interviewer for his or her own perspective on a subject.

After small talk, the interviewer may well begin by telling you about the company, the division, the department, or perhaps the position. Because of your detailed research, information about the company should be already familiar to you. The interviewer will probably like nothing better than to avoid this regurgitation of company history, so if you can do so tactfully, indicate that you're very familiar with the firm. If the interviewer seems determined to provide you with background information despite your hints, then listen attentively. If you can manage to initiate a brief, appropriate discussion of the company or industry at this point, that's great. It will help you to build rapport, underscore your interest, and increase your impact.

Soon the interviewer will begin to ask you questions. This period of the interview may be structured or unstructured, or somewhere in between. In a structured interview, the interviewer asks a prescribed set of questions, seeking relatively brief answers. In the unstructured interview, the interviewer asks more open-ended questions to prod you into giving longer responses and revealing as much as possible about yourself, your background, and your aspirations. Some interviewers will mix both styles, typically beginning with more objective questions and asking more open-ended questions as the interview progresses.

Try to determine as quickly as possible which direction the interviewer is going, and respond to the questions accordingly. As you answer the questions, watch for signals from the employer as to whether your responses are too short or too long. For example, if the employer is nodding or looking away, wrap up your answer as quickly as possible. Following the style the interviewer establishes will make the interview easier and more comfortable and will help you make a more favorable impression.

Once you begin to feel more confident about interviewing, you may wish to think strategically about each interview. One effective tactic is to adjust your speed of speech to match that of the interviewer. People tend to talk at the speed at which they like to be spoken to. If you can adjust your speech rate to that of the recruiter without sounding unnatural, the recruiter will probably feel more comfortable (after all, interviewing others isn't much fun, either) and have a more favorable impression of you.

Another strategy is to adapt your answers to match the type of company for which you're interviewing. For example, if you're interviewing for a job at a large product-marketing company that emphasizes group decision making and spends much of its energy focused on battles for market share with its competitors, you might want to talk about how much you enjoy team sports—especially being part of a team and competing to win.

Concentrate on the themes you've developed in Chapter 1 and be alert for opportunities to mention them. If applicable, draw parallels between your experience and the demands of the position as described by the interviewer. Talk about your past experience, emphasizing results and achievements and not merely recounting activities. If you listen carefully (listening is a crucial part of the interviewing process), the interviewer might very well give you an idea of the skills needed for the position. Don't exaggerate. Be on the level about your abilities.

Try not to be negative about anything during the interview—especially about any past employer or previous job. Be cheerful. Everyone likes to work with someone who seems to be happy.

Don't let a tough question throw you off base. If you don't know the answer to a question, say so simply—don't apologize. Just smile. Nobody can answer every question—particularly some of the questions that are asked in job interviews.

Try not to cover too much ground during the first interview. This interview, in which many candidates are screened out, is often the toughest. If you're interviewing for a very competitive position, you'll have to make an impression that will last. Focus on a few of your greatest strengths that are relevant to the position. Develop these points carefully, state them again in different words, then try to summarize them briefly at the end of the interview.

Above all else, keep the conversation flowing. Don't talk too much or too little; watch the recruiter for signals. A job interview is a conversation between two people who are hoping to discover they have a common interest. Move around if you have to so that you don't appear stiff, but be careful not to fidget. Try to appear relaxed, enthusiastic, and determined—all at the same time!

The First Interview

As mentioned earlier, the first interview is often a screening interview conducted by a human-resources-department representative or an employment interviewer. The types of questions are general in nature—rarely specific to the technical aspects of the job. This is why it's important that you've developed themes related to the most relevant aspects of your own experiences and achievements. (See Chapter 1 for more information on this strategy.)

The primary purpose of the first interview is to determine qualities like motivation, industry or functional skills, work ethic, communication skills, and critical-thinking skills. You should communicate genuine interest in the job, the industry, and the city or region of the country if relocation is part of the package. You need to demonstrate compatibility with the company culture and show that you can sell that compatibility in subsequent interviews if the recruiter moves you to the next round in the process. Recruiters are always concerned about weeding out any candidate who might embarrass them in a second interview; they must believe that they really got to know you and that you won't present any surprises in subsequent interviews. After all, their reputation and judgment are on the line if they recommend you for a second interview.

Strategies for Later Interviews

When filling professional career positions, few companies will make a job offer after only one interview. Usually, the purpose of the first interview is to narrow the field of applicants to a small number of very promising candidates. During the first meeting, then, the ideal strategy is to stand out from a large field of competitors in a positive way. The best way to do this is to emphasize subtly one or two of your key strengths as much as possible throughout the interview.

During later interviews, the competition for the position will drop off, and employers will tend to look not for strengths but for weaknesses. At this point, you should focus on presenting yourself as a well-balanced choice for the position. Listen carefully to the interviewer's questions so you can determine his or her underlying concerns and try to dispel them. On the other hand, if later interviews are primarily with people who are in a position to veto your hiring, but not to push it forward, you should focus primarily on building rapport as opposed to reiterating and developing your key strengths.

Another way in which second interviews differ from first interviews is that the questions become much more specific and technical. The company must now test the depth of your knowledge of the field, including how well you're able to apply your education and past work experience to the job at hand. At this stage, the interviewer isn't a recruiter; you may have one or more interviewers, each of whom has a job related to the one you're applying for. Typically these interviewers will represent your potential boss, professional peer group, or executives who oversee the work group.

The second round of interviews can last one to two days, during which you might meet with as few as several people or as many as fifteen or more over the course of the visit. These interviews typically last longer than initial interviews. For many executive positions, you may also have meetings around breakfast, lunch, or dinner. In all cases, remember you're still in an interview. You may be having a dinner conversation about a recent topic of concern to the industry as a whole—be ready with opinions, and be equally ready to listen and to ask good questions. You may be asked to demonstrate how you'd go about performing some aspect of the job; be ready in case you're presented with a tough problem and asked to tackle it as though you'd already started your first day on the job. Use what you said in the screening interview as an outline (it's gotten you this far!) but be prepared to build on this outline in meaningful ways with more developed details, examples, and ideas.

Usually you can count on attending at least two interviews for most professional positions, or three for high-level positions, though some firms, such as some professional partnerships, are famous for conducting a minimum of six interviews for all professional positions. Though you should be more relaxed as you return for subsequent interviews, the pressure will still be on. The more prepared you are, the better.

Turning the Tables

Often the interviewer will pause toward the end and ask if you have any questions. Particularly in a structured interview, this might be the one chance to communicate your knowledge of, and interest in, the firm. Have a list prepared of specific questions that are of real interest to you. Let your questions subtly show your research and your knowledge of the firm's activities. It's wise to memorize an extensive list of questions, as several of them may be answered during the interview.

When asking the interviewer your questions, follow these guidelines:

- Don't let this opportunity turn into an interrogation. Don't bring your list of questions to the interview.
- Ask questions that you're fairly certain the interviewer can answer. (Remember how you feel when you can't answer a question during an interview.)
- If you're unable to determine the salary range beforehand, don't ask about it during the first interview. You can always ask about it later.
- Don't ask about fringe benefits until you've been offered a position. (Then be sure to get all the details.) You should be able to determine the company's policy on benefits relatively easily before the interview.
- If it looks as though your skills and background don't match the position your interviewer was hoping to fill, ask if there's another division or subsidiary that perhaps could profit from your talents.

What questions should you ask? Here are some examples:

Question: **"What position or positions does this job typically lead to?"**

Question: **"Assuming I was hired and performed well for a number of years, what additional opportunities might this job lead to?"**

These questions imply that you're an achievement-oriented individual looking for a company in which you can build a long-term career.

Question: **"I've noticed in the trade press that your firm has a terrific reputation in marketing. What are the major insights into the marketing process that I might gain from this position?"**

Question: **"I understand that your company is the market leader in industrial drill bits in North America. I'm curious to know how much of the product line is sold overseas—and whether there are many career opportunities in marketing abroad."**

These questions imply that you're very interested in a long-term career in the industry and that you might lean toward pursuing a career with this firm because of its solid reputation. Your well-timed and appropriate questions are sure to impress even the toughest interviewer.

Question: **"What skills are considered most useful for success in the job I'm applying for?"**

This question implies that you really care about your success at your first job, and provides important information you can use to your advantage in the future.

Question: **"I'd really like to work for your firm. I think it's a great company and I'm confident I could do this job well. What's the next step of the selection process?"**

More than a question, this is a powerful statement that will quickly set you apart from other job hunters. However, you should make such a statement only if you mean it. If you're offered the position but then say you need two weeks to think it over, you'll lose your credibility. However, even after responding in this manner, it's reasonable to ask for one or two days to give an offer some thought.

Be sure to save your questions about salary, benefits, and related issues for later, after you receive an offer. You'll still be free to negotiate—or to decline the position—at that point. Also, avoid asking questions that will be difficult or awkward for the recruiter to answer. For example, this is not an appropriate time to ask, "Does your company use recycled paper for all its advertising brochures?"

A Final Note

Interviewing is like almost everything else—the more you do it, the better you become. Don't expect to give a perfect performance—especially in your first few interviews. Even experienced professionals who haven't interviewed in a while are bound to be rusty.

And if you have a terrible interview, don't let it shake your confidence! Remember that everyone has a bad interview experience sooner or later. Learn from it, work on your performance, and keep looking for other opportunities.

PART 2

The Top
250 Questions

Chapter **4**

THE BASIC INTERVIEW QUESTIONS

Okay, now you're ready to start practicing your interview questions. The following are among the most commonly asked questions in interviews today. If you can manage to get a good handle on these, you'll breeze through your interviews and really stand out from the crowd. Remember, employers are often interviewing many people for a single position, so you need to prepare answers that will get you noticed as a winner.

Chances are that a vast majority of the questions you'll be asked on a typical job interview appear in the next two chapters. But you may be asked a variation on one of our questions with different wording. Just remember as you work your way through the next sections that you're not trying to memorize the answers verbatim. Instead you are trying to respond to interview questions in a way that will convey that you're someone the employer would want to hire. In other words, project yourself as someone who's likely to stay with the company for a number of years, who's achievement oriented, who'll fit in well with the other employees, and who's likable. Of course, you should also try to present yourself as someone who's capable of performing extremely well in the position.

You should avoid giving generic answers like "I'm a people person" or "I have excellent written and oral communication skills." Your response should always be specific (with supporting examples), and it should relate specifically to the job, the industry, or other personal factors to help your answer (and you!) stand out. Particularly in screening interviews, where generic questions are often asked, recruiters are looking to eliminate the average respondent. You can't afford a predictable, nondescript response. You must turn a common question into a memorable answer.

Go through the practice interview questions in the next two chapters. At first you may wish to read the sample responses and the accompanying discussion. Later, as you begin to feel more comfortable with the questions, try answering them without any help, as you would during a real interview.

1. Passion for the Business

Question 1: **Why do you want to work in this industry?**

Answer: I've always wanted to work in an industry that makes tools. One of my hobbies is home-improvement projects, so I've collected a number of saws manufactured by your company. I could be an accountant anywhere, but I'd rather work for a company whose products I trust.

Tell a story about how you first became interested in this type of work. Point out any similarities between the job you're interviewing for and your current or most recent job. Provide proof that you aren't simply shopping in this interview. Make your passion for your work a theme that you allude to continually throughout the interview.

Question 2: **Why would you be particularly good at this business?**

Answer: I was a pastry chef, so I understand dessert products well and can help you with new product development. Recent preservatives have come a long way toward eliminating texture difference in pastry dough. This means we can investigate many more products than before.

Show how you keep up due to natural inquisitiveness, reading, and so on. Do you have sufficient natural interest to go that extra step and channel appropriate energy into your work? Give a specific answer.

Question 3: **How do you stay current?**

Answer: I pore over the *Wall Street Journal*, the *Times*, *Institutional Investor*, and several mutual fund newsletters that are published online. And I have a number of friends who are analysts.

Demonstrate natural interest in the industry or career field by describing publications or trade associations that are compatible with your goal.

Question 4: **Why do you think this industry would sustain your interest over the long haul?**

Answer: The technology in the industry is changing so rapidly that I see lots of room for job enhancement regardless of promotions. I'm particularly interested in the many applications for multimedia as a training tool.

What expectations or projections do you have for the business that would enable you to grow without necessarily advancing? What excites you about the business? What proof can you offer that your interest has already come from a deep curiosity—perhaps going back at least a few years—rather than a current whim you'll outgrow?

Question 5: **Where do you want to be in five years?**

Answer: I'd like to have the opportunity to work in a plant as well as at the home office. I also hope to develop my management skills, perhaps by managing a small staff.

Don't give specific time frames or job titles. Talk about what you enjoy, skills that are natural to you, realistic problems or opportunities you'd expect in your chosen field or industry, and what you hope to learn from those experiences. You shouldn't discuss your goals in a field or industry unrelated to the job you're applying for. This may sound obvious, but too many job candidates make this mistake, unwittingly demonstrating a real lack of interest in their current field or industry. Needless to say, such a gaffe will immediately eliminate you from further consideration.

Question 6: **Describe your ideal career.**

Answer: I'd like to stay in a field related to training no matter what happens. I was too interested in business to work at a university, but I believe that teaching is somehow in my blood. I've been good at sales because I took the time to educate my clients. Now I look forward to training the new hires.

Talk about what you enjoy, skills that are natural to you, realistic problems or opportunities you'd expect in this particular job or industry, and what you hope to learn from those experiences. Avoid mentioning specific time frames or job titles.

Question 7: **If you had unlimited time and financial resources, how would you spend them?**

Answer: I'd love to be able to take several executive seminars on financial management that aren't geared toward financial experts. I'd also love to be able to shut down my department long enough to send everyone through an Outward Bound–type program. Finally,

I'd probably travel and look at foreign competitors, and enjoy the food along the way. What would you do?

Although it's tempting to discuss things you'd do for fun, stick to job- or industry-related pursuits, or to skill-building efforts that could transfer to the job you're applying for. For example, if you're applying for a teaching job, you might also be interested in volunteering for an adult literacy program; this demonstrates a belief in the importance of education even without pay as an incentive.

2. Motivation and Purpose

Question 8: **Tell me something about yourself that I didn't know from reading your resume.**

Answer: You wouldn't know that I've managed my own small portfolio since I was sixteen, but I believe that it's important for you to understand my interest in investment sales. I've averaged a 12 percent return over the past eight years.

Don't just repeat what's on your resume. Think of a talent or skill that didn't quite fit into your employment history, but that's unique and reveals something intriguing about your personality or past experience.

Question 9: **Tell me what you know about this company.**

Answer: I served as an intern to a restaurant analyst last summer, so I followed all the steak-house chains closely. What you've done especially well is focus on a limited menu with great consistency among locations; the business traveler trusts your product anywhere in the U.S. I'm particularly interested in your real-estate finance group and expansion plans.

Describe your first encounter or a recent encounter with the company or its products and services. What would be particularly motivating to you about working there as opposed to working the same type of job in a different company? The recruiter will look for evidence of genuine interest and more than just surface research on the company. Reciting the annual report isn't likely to impress most recruiters, but feedback from customers and employees will.

Question 10: **What have you learned about our company from customers, employees, or others?**

Answer: I actually called several of the key accounts mentioned in your brochure. Two of the customers I spoke with explained why they continued to buy from you year after year. Your distribution operation is phenomenal. Are there any service improvements you think could still be made?

Describe how your interest has grown from personal dealings with company representatives. Think creatively in preparing for job interviews. For example, prior to your job interview, speak with retailers or workers at other distribution points about the company's product line. What can they tell you? Give one or two examples of what you've learned to explain why you're interested in this company. What's the most compelling example you can describe to prove your interest?

Question 11: **Why do you want to work here?**

Answer: I lost a bid several years ago to your company. I realized then that products in the computer industry are becoming increasingly similar. They're so similar now, and retail prices are so competitive, that service is the best way for a company to distinguish itself from the competition. This company has the best service record of all its competitors, and I believe it will dominate the business in the long run.

Your preparation and research should become apparent here. Give one or two reasons why you're interested in the company, and what in particular piqued your interest. What's the most compelling thing you can describe about your personal experience with the company, its products, or its employees? Possible answers include the company's reputation, the job description itself, or a desire to get involved with the industry.

Question 12: **What particular aspect of the company interests you most?**

Answer: I'm most interested in your Latin American developments. My father was an army officer, so we lived for three years in Latin America. I know you've just entered joint ventures with two processing companies there. What are your plans for the next few years?

This is another opportunity for you to showcase your special knowledge of the company. If you did the proper research, as described in Chapter 1, you should have no problem answering this question.

Question 13: **What's your favorite product made by our company?**

Answer: I've used Softer Than Ever shampoo for years. In fact, my initial contact with the company was the brand manager for Softer Than Ever. She encouraged me to apply for an HR position here.

Describe personal use—why do you use the company's products? What do you think are new market opportunities for that product?

Question 14: **What do you think of our newest product and ads?**

Answer: It seems that your new ads are trying to show that breakfast time is family time, with a certain wholesomeness. Are you doing this to balance against the recent bad press about high-fat foods, without attacking the issue directly?

You should be familiar enough with the company's new products and advertising campaigns to make informed, intelligent comments about them. Offer specific suggestions and positive comments.

Question 15: **Tell me what you think our distinctive advantage is within the industry.**

Answer: With your low-cost-producer status and headquarters operation in a low-cost area of the country, you seem in a better position to be able to spend aggressively on R&D, even in a down year, compared to your closest rival.

Describe things you believe the company does very well, particularly compared to its competition. Explain how the financial strength of the company is important.

Question 16: **Where do you think we're the most vulnerable as a business?**

Answer: Your cash position and strong product presence make you an attractive target for a takeover. That's my only major concern. I've already worked for one organization that merged with another, but I also know I can weather the storm.

Describe things you believe the company does not do well compared to its competition. Explain how the company's financial strength is important. If you've a passion for the business, the future of the job is probably always on your mind.

Question 17: **What would you do differently if you ran the company?**

Answer: I might investigate whether to sell off the light-manufacturing businesses and start an aggressive supplier-relations program.

In a constructive way demonstrate that you have enough knowledge about the business to answer this question convincingly. One way to gain such knowledge is by talking to a sufficient number of company insiders, which is why this question can quickly weed out the "shoppers" from more serious job candidates. You can also turn the question around—ask for the recruiter's ideas, too. You might learn something valuable.

Question 18:   **What other firms are you interviewing with, and for what positions?**

Answer: Actually, I've definitely decided to pursue a career as a restaurant manager, so I'm applying only for restaurant management–training programs. I've recently had interviews with several other large national fast-food chains, such as Super Burger and Clackey's Chicken.

Often the candidate will try to impress the employer by naming some large firms in unrelated industries with completely different types of jobs. This is a big mistake! What employers want to hear is that you're interviewing for similar jobs in the same industry at similar firms (such as their competitors). This illustrates that you're committed to finding a job in your field of interest and are likely to be a low-risk hire.

Question 19:   **Do you believe you're overqualified for this position?**

Answer: Not at all. My experience and qualifications make me do my job only better, and in my opinion, my good design skills help to sell more books. My business experience helps me run the art department in a cost-efficient manner, thus saving the company money. Finally, I think I'm able to attract better freelance talent because of all my industry contacts. My qualifications are better for the company, too, since you'll be getting a better return for your investment. Again, I'm interested in establishing a long-term relationship with my employer, and if I did well, I would expect expanded responsibilities that could make use of even other skills.

Most people don't expect to be asked if they have a great deal of experience. This question could quite easily catch a candidate off guard, which is exactly the interviewer's intention. The candidate doesn't hesitate in answering this question and shows complete confidence in his or her ability.

Question 20: **Describe our competition as you see it.**

Answer: Most of your competitors have tried to do too many things. As a result, most have had difficulty expanding and maintaining consistent quality.

Give evidence that you've researched the company and industry carefully and acquired more than superficial knowledge. Point out positive and/or negative aspects of the company's competitors. Discuss how the company's initiatives are better suited to your personal interests.

Question 21: **What would you do if one of our competitors offered you a position?**

Answer: I'd say no. I'm not interested in other players in this industry. I want to work for Nike because I won a number of races wearing the Nike brand. Because of my positive experience with Nike, I know I'd be convincing selling your product to retailers.

The interviewer is trying to determine whether the candidate is truly interested in the industry and company, or whether he or she has chosen the company randomly. Contrast your perceptions of the company with its competitors, and talk about the company's products or services that you've encountered. In the long run, which players do you believe are most viable and why? This is also a good place to ask the interviewer for his or her opinion.

Question 22: **Why are you ready to leave your current job?**

Answer: My interest lies in returning to the banking industry. I can work in human-resources management in many environments, but I believe that my experience as a lender prepares me exceptionally well for recruiting new lenders into the training program.

Give two or three reasons why you're ready to leave your current job. Focus on limitations in growth, or lack of challenge, in your current job. Make sure you point out why you believe the position you're interviewing for would provide the challenge and additional responsibilities that you desire.

Question 23: **What do you want out of your next job?**

Answer: I'm really interested in taking over a territory where we aren't very well positioned. My sales successes to date have been in areas where we already had a decent market share. I also want a very aggressive commission structure if I'm able to turn around a problem territory.

This question is similar to "Why are you ready to leave your current job?" Give one or two examples from your current work experience that explain why you're interviewing for the position. Focus on your desire for greater challenge. For example, "I've gone as far as I can go in my current job unless someone vacates a position." Make sure you point out why you believe the job at hand provides the additional responsibilities you're seeking.

Question 24:   **What's your dream job?**

Answer: My dream job would include all of the responsibilities and duties in this position you're trying to fill. I also thrive in a fast-changing environment where there's business growth. Your plans call for expanding internationally during the next year, and this would satisfy one of my ultimate goals of being involved in an international corporation.

This is your ideal chance to sell your aptitudes that fit the job description. Show an interest in finding new ways these skills can be put to use in a new job with additional responsibilities. Tie in the industry, size of the company, or other factors where appropriate.

Question 25:   **What motivates you to do this kind of work?**

Answer: I've been fortunate in my own schooling; I had wonderful teachers. I want to be that same kind of teacher—who not only encourages kids to learn but also sets an example that inspires others to want to teach. In the long run, that's our best chance of turning around the quality of education in this state.

The interviewer will want to know about your belief in the products or services of the company. Use personal experience to demonstrate your interests and strengths. In an interview for your ideal job, you'd be highly motivated to get paid for working at something you liked. The interviewer will want to know if your natural interests are compatible with this particular job.

Question 26:   **What salary would you expect for this job?**

Answer: Based on your job description, which mentions that you prefer someone with a master's degree in engineering, I hope you consider the fact that my skills meet your highest standards.

Therefore, I'd expect a salary at the high end of your pay range for the position classification. Can you give me some indication of your range?

Recruiters want to weed out people whose financial goals are unrealistic. This question is a direct hit—it forces a response about a touchy subject. If you mention a salary that's too low, you may seem uninformed; too high, and you may outprice yourself or ruin your ability to bargain. It's best to turn the question back on the recruiter. Ask what the salary range is for the position; then ask the recruiter to consider how your qualifications rate compared to the average requirements for the position.

Question 27: **What new skills or ideas do you bring to the job that other candidates aren't likely to offer?**

Answer: Because I've worked with the oldest player in this industry, I can help you avoid some of the mistakes we made in our established markets. I think that retaining your core customer base is more important than securing new accounts right now.

This question addresses the candidate's motivation for adding "true value" (beyond what's expected) to the job. Have you thought about the job carefully, considering current limitations or weaknesses in the current department and your unique abilities? If you're running neck and neck with another candidate, your ability here to prove "I offer what you need and then some" could land you the job.

Question 28: **What interests you most about this job?**

Answer: I'd love the opportunity to work with John Doe, whom I watched build the financial-services practice under bank deregulation. I think our utilities clients will go through a lot of the same problems that banks faced in the eighties. John's insights will be sound, and John and I have worked well together on several projects.

Point out the new experiences you look forward to in the job as well as reasons you believe you're uniquely suited to the position. Point out similarities to some of your past jobs in which you enjoyed success.

Question 29: **What would you like to accomplish that you weren't able to accomplish in your last position?**

Answer: I was hampered by a small budget that limited our marketing efforts to print ads and other traditional resources. I'd like to explore interactive media, because the eight-to-twenty-five-year-old category responds to computer-based media.

This question should be answered in the same way you'd answer "Why are you ready to leave your current job?" Remain positive—discuss things you enjoy and have an aptitude for, but avoid dwelling on the limitations of your last job.

Question 30: **We have a number of applicants interviewing for this position. Why should we take a closer look at you?**

Answer: I'm probably one of the few CPAs you'll find who's worked in two Hispanic countries. With all the production that you're outsourcing to Mexico, I may be able to provide some assistance with your inventory planning.

This is similar to the question "Why should I hire you?" What's the most compelling item you can describe to prove your qualifications and interest? Is there something extra you offer besides the basic job qualifications? Be specific in your answer. Whatever answer you prepare, try using it when you wrap up the interview, if you haven't yet been asked this question.

Question 31: **How have your career motivations changed over the past few years?**

Answer: When I started in sales, I didn't realize how much I'd miss it if I left. Now I want to stay close to the field organization, even though I'm looking at marketing jobs. Your firm attracts me because the account-team concept would keep me in tune with customer needs.

Describe what you've learned from your past jobs, especially where your skills and natural instincts have become apparent. Your current motivation should relate strongly to the job you're interviewing for.

Question 32:   **Why should I hire you?**

Answer: My uncle had a company that was a small-scale manufacturer in the industry, and although he later sold the business, I worked there for five summers doing all sorts of odd jobs. For that reason I believe I know this business from the ground up, and you can be assured that I know what I'd be getting into as a plant manager here.

Don't repeat your resume or employment history. Offer one or two examples to explain why you're talking to this particular company. What's the most compelling example you can give to prove your interest? This question often remains unasked, but it's always in the back of a recruiter's mind. Even if this question isn't asked, you should find an opportunity to use your prepared response sometime during the interview, perhaps in your closing remarks.

3. Skills and Experience

Question 33:   **What are your key skills?**

Answer: After working six years as a senior systems analyst, I've developed a number of key skills, including business modeling, process re-engineering, software-package evaluation, and excellent programming skills in UNIX and C environments. I was very pleased to discover that these are the skills you're seeking. Do you want to hear about specific examples of my work?

Talk about your key skills and how you'll use them in this job. Avoid clichés or generalities. Offer specific evidence, drawing parallels from your current or previous job to the job you're interviewing for.

Question 34: **What sets you apart from the crowd?**

Answer: Once I'm committed to a job or a project, I tackle it with tremendous intensity. I want to learn everything I can, and my goal is to achieve results beyond the expectations of my supervisor. I guess you might say I'm very competitive and like to excel at everything I do.

Your answer should communicate self-confidence, but avoid sounding arrogant. Talk about observations other people have made about your work, talents, or successes.

Question 35: **What are your strengths?**

Answer: My strengths are interpersonal skills, and I can usually win people over to my point of view. Also, I have good judgment about people and an intuitive sense of their talents and their ability to contribute to a given problem. These skills seem to me directly related to the job. I notice that you require three years' work experience for this job. Although my resume shows that I've only two years' experience, it doesn't show that I took two evening college courses related to my field and have been active in one of the professional societies. I also try to gain knowledge by reading the industry's trade journals. I'm certain that my combined knowledge and skill level is the equivalent of that of other people who actually do have three years' work experience. I'm also currently enrolled in a time-management course; I can already see the effects of this course at work on my present job.

Describe two or three skills you have that are most relevant to the job. Avoid clichés or generalities; offer specific evidence. Describe new ways these skills could be put to use in the new position. If you have to talk about weaknesses, be honest without shooting yourself in the foot—avoid pointing out a weakness that might be a major obstacle to landing the job. For example, it might be wise to mention that you barely have the required work experience for the job; the interviewer has surely noticed this much, and then you can explain how you're qualified for the job nonetheless.

Question 36: **How is your experience relevant to this job?**

Answer: In my current job I've recently completed three re-engineering projects. I gathered all the necessary market data, developed a benchmarking program, and put together a team to do the evaluation and analysis. As a result I'm ready to tackle the major re-engineering project that you've listed as the priority of this job during the first year. In my past job I was the liaison between the project engineering group and the instrumentation group in the testing of a new turbo engine. This experience will also help me tackle this job, which involves a close and careful working relationship between your technical group and your field-testing group.

Draw parallels from your current or previous job to the require-ments of this job. A similarity that seems obvious to you may not be so obvious to the recruiter. Ask questions about the job, if necessary, to get the interviewer to accept your rationale.

Question 37: **What skills do you think are most critical to this job?**

Answer: The ability to evaluate all of the regulatory and com-petitive requirements for your new product are critical. I've had considerable experience in this area as a strategic-marketing and regulatory-policy analyst in my most recent job, and also in my first job.

Describe the immediate relevance of your past experience. Draw parallels from your current or previous job to the requirements of this job.

Question 38: **What skills would you like to develop in this job?**

Answer: I'd like to develop my negotiating skills. I've had considerable experience interpreting and implementing large contracts, but I've been limited in negotiating the actual conditions, costs, and standards for a major contract. I believe this job will offer me the opportunity to be a member of a negotiating team and thereby to begin acquiring the skills necessary to lead the team.

Describe several aptitudes you haven't been able to develop fully in your current job. For example, your opportunity to manage the department might have been hindered because your supervisor plans to stay in his or her job at least five more years.

Question 39: **If you had to stay in your current job, what would you spend more time on? Why?**

Answer: If I stay in my current job, I'd like to gain more experience in labor negotiating. In particular, I'd like to help negotiate labor contracts, resolve grievances at the step-4 level, and prepare grievances for arbitration. My background in all other areas of human resources is strong, and I believe labor-relations experience will round out my skills so that I can have the opportunity to move up as a department head or a vice president in the future.

What interests you most about your job? Describe the responsibilities that give you the most satisfaction. In addition, show a real interest in upgrading the job, staying on the leading edge, and so on.

Question 40: **How could you enrich your current job?**

Answer: When I was a research assistant for the cable and wireless company back in ninety-three, at a time when we were experiencing rapid growth, our pricing analyst abruptly resigned for a better job. During the search to fill his position, I volunteered to help out with one of the major government projects. I worked considerable overtime, studied on my own, and helped bring the project to conclusion. I was commended for my effort and was told I'd be in line for the next opening in the pricing group.

Show an ability to add value continually to your job. What new opportunities exist that could challenge your skills and intellect? The interviewer will want to feel confident that you won't get bored or disenchanted with your work.

Question 41: **How do you explain your job successes?**

Answer: I never assume our customers are satisfied with our product, so I do my best to follow up with every customer. This feedback has provided valuable insight into the quality and characteristics of our products. The customer, as well, always appreciates this follow-up, especially when something hasn't gone right and you still have the opportunity to correct it on a timely basis. In addition, I'm able to pass on information to our design and production units to help improve both process and product.

Be candid without sounding arrogant. Mention observations other people have made about your work strengths or talents. This question is similar to the question "What sets you apart from the crowd?"

Question 42: **Compared to others with a similar background in your field, how would you rate yourself?**

Answer: I've been consistently ranked in the top 10 percent nationally for all salespeople in my field. I sell advertising space for a national news publication. My clients are primarily large ad agencies that represent corporate America. I've always enjoyed the challenge of selling to advertising-agency executives because they always set high standards and really know our product well. This brings out the very best in my competitive nature, and I'm consistently at the top, both within my publishing company and within the industry.

Be honest and self-confident without sounding arrogant. Give clear, convincing reasons for your answer. If you've been in the top 10 percent in sales nationally, this is a good time to bring it up!

Question 43: **How good are your writing abilities?**

Answer: I really concentrated on further developing my writing skills while I got my M.B.A. I took an entrepreneurial class in which the chief assignment was developing, writing, and continually rewriting a very involved business plan.

This is an excellent answer. Have a business plan or something similar ready to show the recruiter. Leave your business plan with the recruiter after the interview. The recruiter will be looking for a candidate with writing ability, especially for jobs where a lot of writing is required, like for financial analysts or copywriters.

Question 44: **What computer systems and software do you know?**

Answer: I've used PCs with general-office software such as Microsoft Word, PowerPoint, InDesign, and Excel. I have some experience with Macintosh systems as well. And through my search for a computer network, I've gained some familiarity with local networks; the computer company we used trained me on basic troubleshooting issues.

In today's business environment, computer literacy is a must. Word-processing and spreadsheet experience is essential, and familiarity with database management or graphics programs is valuable as well. Most businesses use PC-compatible computers, but many companies in the creative field, such as publishing or advertising, use Macintosh computers. If you're interviewing in one of those fields, you might find it helpful to familiarize yourself with Macs.

4. Diligence and Professionalism

Question 45:   **Give an example of how you saw a project through, despite obstacles.**

Answer: I actually rotated off an account but kept my hand in it as an adviser, because the client had threatened to pull the account if he wasn't dealing with me. Over three months I was able to make the client more comfortable with my replacement while I slowly decreased my presence.

Demonstrate how you gather resources and foresee and manage obstacles. Focus your answer on the solution and execution, not on the obstacles themselves.

Question 46:   **Share an example of your determination.**

Answer: I led an effort to change our production system over to dedicated lines. The biggest problem was convincing the factory workers that this strategy made sense, even though they'd have to learn to do their jobs differently. I assured them that within a few months their jobs would be easier, and we'd save about four man-hours per employee per week. I convinced management to increase the profit-sharing account using half of those savings, which also helped get the employees on my side.

Describe a time you persevered to accomplish a goal. A personal goal (for example, one that reflects an interest in developing a new skill) would be appropriate here. Demonstrate how you gather resources, predict obstacles, and manage stress.

Question 47: **Share an example of your diligence or perseverance.**

Answer: About halfway through our last system installation, the client changed her requirements. Our partner agreed that, at the new costs the client would incur, we could still meet the original completion date. It took about seventy to eighty hours a week for us to get the job done, but we did it, knowing that it would be over within three months.

Describe your professional character, including thoroughness, diligence, and accountability. Demonstrate how you gather resources, use time-management techniques, or go the extra mile. Use a specific example.

Question 48: **Describe a time when you tackled a tough or unpopular assignment.**

Answer: I had to determine which budgets would be cut within my division to yield an overall 5 percent cost reduction. I tried to remain objective and keep the personalities of department heads out of the decision. Ultimately, I ended up getting each department head to commit to a .25 percent reduction through frugal travel-expense planning, which was an enormous part of our sales division's costs. We accomplished most of the savings by combining trips and by securing two-week-advance airline reservations whenever possible.

Describe a time you were willing, or even volunteered, to solve a problem that had remained unresolved after earlier attempts. Or describe something you accomplished that was important to the company's long-term interests, even if short-term implications were less than favorable. Your answer might involve a problem employee or a process-improvement plan, for example.

Question 49: **Would your current boss describe you as the kind of employee who goes the extra mile?**

Answer: Absolutely. In fact, on my annual evaluations she writes that I'm the most dependable and flexible person on her staff. I think this is mostly because of my ability to juggle and prioritize. Would you like an example?

Be ready to offer proof that you persevere to see important projects through and to achieve important results. Share an example that demonstrates your dependability or willingness to tackle a tough project. If you describe "long hours of work," make sure you demonstrate that the hours were productive, and not the result of poor time management.

Question 50: **How many days were you absent from work last year? Why?**

Answer: I was absent four days last year, three because I came down with the flu, and once due to the death of a family member.

A history of absenteeism or tardiness, or any indication of a weak work ethic or poor performance standards, can be detrimental to you. Convince the interviewer of your willingness to take responsibility at work, and of your punctuality, dependability, and solid attendance record. If you think you may get poor references because of attendance or undependability, you'd better be well prepared to give a detailed and exonerating explanation. A similar question you may be asked is "Are you punctual?"

Question 51: **Tell me about a time you didn't perform to your capabilities.**

Answer: The first time I had to give a presentation to our board, I failed to anticipate some of their questions. I was unprepared for anything other than what I wanted to report. Now my director and I brainstorm all the what-ifs in advance.

This question forces the candidate to describe a negative situation. Do so in the context of an early career mistake based on inexperience; then demonstrate the better judgment you now have as a result of that learning experience.

Question 52: **Employees tend to be either concept oriented or task oriented. How do you describe yourself?**

Answer: It's important for me to have clear direction on each project. That's why I'm good in support roles, with managers who have very specific ideas. I'm thorough at carrying out the tasks.

With this question the interviewer looks for a match between the candidate's preferred level of detail and the level of detail required by the job. Problems might arise if the job requires delegation but the candidate enjoys working independently. When you've completed projects in the past, have you performed within the scope of the task assigned?

Question 53: **What would your colleagues tell me about your attention to detail?**

Answer: My coworkers always count on me to help them think through what might have been overlooked, so they'd probably tell you I think through processes from A to Z.

Here the interviewer is interested in the candidate's dependability and follow-through. Are you responsible? Have you contributed productively to a team effort without getting caught up in unnecessary detail? Do you use your time efficiently? If you do, mention specific praise given by one of your peers.

Question 54: **How do you manage stress in your daily work?**

Answer: I try to get out for lunch at least once during the week to clear my head. I also have a personal rule that stops me from reacting to any problem until I feel calm about it. I think, then act—but I've learned to do that over time.

It might be helpful here to describe a stressful project you've worked on and the specific actions you took to organize each step and see the project through. How do you keep yourself calm and professional under pressure?

Question 55: **How do you regroup when things haven't gone as planned?**

Answer: I start by trying to imagine the worst possible outcome; then I back up and identify precautions I can take to avoid that scenario. In this way I usually end up with a result close to the original goal. The training example I described earlier is proof of that skill.

Describe a time when some obstacle forced you to change your original plan, but you were still able to achieve the desired result. Did you rally the support of others to make this happen? With hindsight, how might you have better predicted the obstacle?

Question 56: **How have you prioritized or juggled your workload in your current job?**

Answer: I juggle by working only on my two major accounts early in the day. That way, if interruptions occur, my most critical customers are taken care of.

Demonstrate how you gather resources, how you predict obstacles, and how you manage stress. Describe personal habits that allow you to move ahead on priorities and avoid micromanaging or putting out fires. In what ways have you become better at managing time over the years?

Question 57: **Describe a professional skill you've developed in your most recent job.**

Answer: I'm most proud of my new skills in applying database technology—for example, in our mailing services. What used to take us days of manual sorting now takes five minutes through a quick-search feature.

Describe a skill you've improved in order to manage your work more efficiently. Typical examples might include learning a new software application, taking a professional seminar, or taking adult-education classes.

Question 58: **Why is service such an important issue?**

Answer: Service is a major contributor to customer satisfaction. Just as important as, or maybe even more important than, cost. If a customer isn't receiving a level of service that meets or exceeds his or her expectations, that customer won't be a customer for very long. In addition, that customer's experience with your company may affect how potential customers in the marketplace view your company. People do talk and share information. This may affect not only profits but future sales as well. In many instances service may be the one thing that distinguishes a company from the competition. A bad reputation for service may compromise a company's position in the marketplace.

The interviewer is trying to determine if the candidate understands the importance of customer service in establishing a positive image in the marketplace, and its impact on new business sales. Outstanding customer service is also a great help in establishing long-term clients and repeat business—the profitable company's bread and butter. The longer the relationship, the greater the possibility for profit.

Question 59: **Tell me about a time when you had to deal with an irate customer. How did you handle the situation?**

Answer: My customer service position at the company involved dealing occasionally with irate customers. When that happened, I'd try to talk in a calm, even voice, in order to get the person to respond in a businesslike manner and focus on trying to resolve the situation. Most times I was able to rectify the problem and pacify the customer, but I remember one incident in particular in which the caller became verbally abusive. I tried to remain calm and professional and not to let my personal feelings enter into the situation. I didn't respond to the abuse, I just made a note of it and continued to help the customer as best I could. When the abuse persisted, however, I politely asked him to call back and ask for my manager, because at that point I knew I couldn't resolve the problem.

How you react when others lose their temper or become upset is very important in most positions, especially in service industries. The interviewer will be looking for evidence of your aptitude for work that involves a great deal of contact with the public. Give an example of a time when you were faced with a difficult person and how you handled it. Your answer should illustrate your maturity, diplomacy, and awareness of the needs and feelings of others.

Question 60: **Are there any issues from your personal life that might have an impact on your professional career?**

Answer: I'm always careful to separate my personal life from my professional life. I believe it's important to remain objective when treating patients. A therapist should always be able to take an emotional step back in order to make an unbiased assessment of a patient. It only hurts the patient when you try to project your own issues and feelings onto that patient.

This question is especially important to those in the health-service fields. The interviewer wants to determine how well you've integrated yourself as an individual. If you have personal issues that you've been unable to work through, they could easily interfere with your relationships with your patients. These issues could also affect your judgment in assessing patients, as well as how you approach treatment planning and recommendations. Assure the interviewer that you can sort out personal opinions from professional behavior. For instance, if you've experienced a crisis that you haven't dealt with positively, you might not be willing to help your patients face really traumatic issues because that would bring up too many of your own intense emotions.

Question 61: **When have your skills in diplomacy been put to the test?**

Answer: A customer came in once and demanded money back for an evening dress that had apparently been worn. She claimed it was a different color after dry cleaning and that the cleaner said the fabric was faulty. I quickly told her we'd happily return her money, even though I didn't think she was being honest. I decided it was more important to keep other customers from hearing her and maybe doubting our high-quality merchandise.

Describe a problem situation with a client or a work associate that you resolved by remaining objective. How did you show empathy and build rapport?

Question 62: **How do you manage your work week and make realistic deadlines?**

Answer: I always reserve two hours of dead time every day to handle any unanticipated problems that may occur. I used to plan for eight or nine hours of project time, but now I find that I'm able to manage my own projects, as well as whatever my boss and staff need from me.

To answer this question effectively, describe in detail how you establish priorities, set deadlines, and determine schedules.

Question 63: **Tell me about a time you had to extend a deadline.**

Answer: Two weeks into a job, it was clear that our client expected us to add more features as we went along. I renegotiated with the client, outlined his goals, and showed him a price structure similar to a menu, from which he could choose more features at a higher cost and in a longer time frame. He opted for something in the middle that he understood would cause a three-week adjustment to the schedule.

Describe your accountability and willingness to adjust a deadline in order to satisfy the overall goals of a project. Had you not adjusted the deadline, what goal would have been compromised?

Question 64: **What personal skill or work habit have you struggled to improve?**

Answer: I had to learn to say no. I used to be helpful to the point that other staff abused my goodwill. Now I offer to help by countering with something I'd like help on in return. On balance I believe the trade-off is more equitable, and cooperation in our office has improved over time.

This question is similar to "Describe a professional skill you've developed in your most recent job." However, here you probably want to discuss an improvement from the earliest days of your career or from your relatively distant past. Make sure you convince the interviewer that this particular work habit is no longer an obstacle.

Question 65: **What books do you keep on your desk?**

Answer: I keep a good dictionary on my desk. I also keep Strunk and White, which is a good reference for looking up all the grammar rules that you learned in high school and college but forgot, or for particularly difficult situations.

The recruiter will be interested in determining how seriously you take your profession. A good dictionary and a good reference book are typical, and necessary, books for a writer to keep on hand. Perhaps you like to keep your favorite novel on your desk as well.

5. Creativity and Leadership

Question 66: **What color is your brain?**

Answer: My brain is red because I'm always hot. I'm always on fire with new plans and ideas.

Be aware that you'll probably be asked zany questions. The point is not to stump you, but to find out what makes you tick. When the standard interview questions are asked, people are prepared, and it's harder for the recruiter to get to know the real person. An advertising recruiter, for example, tries to avoid this. There is no right or wrong answer to this type of question. In fact, the recruiter won't even really care what your answer is. He or she just doesn't want to hear something like, "I don't know, I guess it's blue because that's the way I imagine it." The point is to see how creative you are and how you think. Be sure to explain why you answered the way that you did.

Question 67: **If you got on an elevator where everyone was facing the back, what would you do?**

Answer: I think I'd face the front anyway and say aloud, "It's really much more comfortable facing forward, you know."

Interviews in creative fields like advertising and graphic design are different from other types of job interviews. Advertising recruiters tend to have a different interview style and process, usually conducting more of a behavioral interview. Recruiters ask questions like these to figure out what your behavior might be in a particular real-life situation.

Question 68: **What's the most creative or innovative project you've worked on?**

Answer: During my summer job at Cellular One, I noticed that the sales inquiries were distributed haphazardly to all the marketing assistants in the office. I decided to set up a system grouping inquiries according to region or according to company size. This approach enabled the entire marketing team to come up with better and more creative solutions to our sales problems.

Provide examples of your initiative and resourcefulness. Discuss how your leadership skills have helped you accomplish your goals. Give a specific example that shows a creative, new, or unusual approach to reaching your goals.

Question 69: **Describe a time when you've creatively overcome an obstacle.**

Answer: My publishing company could never get an appointment with a major Fortune 500 company. After several sales representatives gave up in frustration, I volunteered to take a crack at the account. Instead of contacting the vice president of advertising,

I decided to target the VP's administrative assistant. I scheduled an appointment with the assistant and gave him my sales pitch. I really made an impression, because the assistant convinced the vice president that she should schedule an appointment with me. In fact, she penciled me in on her calendar on the spot. I had the appointment, and we got the order two weeks later.

In answer to this question, it's often helpful to focus on how you overcome problems by rallying the support of your coworkers. How have you approached a problem differently from how others might have addressed the same problem? Emphasize your creative solution and its positive results.

Question 70:   **Consider the following scenario: You're working late one evening and are the last person in the office. You answer an urgent telephone call to your supervisor from a sales rep who's currently meeting with a potential client. The sales rep needs an answer to a question to close the sale. Tomorrow will be too late. You have the expertise to answer the question, but it's beyond your normal level of authority. How would you respond?**

Answer: I'd get all the pertinent information, taking well-documented notes. I'd then answer the question based on my knowledge and the information provided. I'd leave my supervisor a note and fill him or her in on the details the next morning. I'd be sure to explain my decision, as well as the thought process behind it.

This response shows that the candidate is confident in his or her ability and can be counted on in an emergency. Similarly, your answer should indicate that you're not afraid to be the decision maker in a tough situation, even if the situation's beyond your normal level of authority.

Question 71: **Why do you think that some companies with good products fail?**

Answer: Employees who are involved in the design and/or manufacture of a product must totally understand and believe in the product and use it on a regular basis. Only in this way can they continually modify and improve it to the customer's satisfaction. Any product must be constantly fine-tuned to meet the changing needs and demands of the consumer. Only by getting the employees involved with the product and excited about it can this improvement occur.

This is a question about the candidate's vision as a leader. If you're asked this question, you'll do well to discuss a specific example of a product or idea that failed because of poor enthusiasm from employees or other consumers. Without being overly critical, you should discuss what you would have done differently.

Question 72: **How resourceful are you?**

Answer: At one time, for all of our new product launches, our chief engineer would release a press statement about its virtues. But when I was given responsibility for a new launch, I decided to get three of our largest customers to videotape an endorsement for use in our marketing campaign. The result was a far higher level of credibility, and we exceeded our six-month sales quota. We now use personal endorsements routinely when we launch our products.

This is a question about the candidate's creativity and initiative. Provide an example of how you've changed your plan or direction and achieved the same, or a better, result. You might want to focus on how you obtained crucial information or how you changed your personal style to get someone to cooperate.

Question 73:   **Give me proof of your persuasiveness.**

Answer: During my summer internship I was assigned the task of conducting a benchmarking study for all the communication expenditures for a major utility. I had to get the consensus of employees in several different departments. Unfortunately, they resented the fact that I was just a summer intern, and they refused to cooperate. I had to schedule individual meetings with every employee and persuade each one that what I was doing would be ultimately beneficial to his or her own department and to the company. After a frustrating month I finally got everyone's cooperation, the project went flawlessly, and in the end I received a bonus for my efforts.

This is a question about leadership, but try not to use an example in which you were the designated leader. If possible, describe a time when you didn't really have authority but instead used your powers of persuasion to get people on your side. Describe your goal and the outcome of your efforts. Why did people trust or believe you?

Question 74:   **What would your last supervisor say about your initiative?**

Answer: In any job I hold I can usually find inefficiencies in a process, and I always try to take some initiative to come up with a solution for improvement. My last supervisor was a little surprised and flustered the first few months when I was constantly coming to him with my ideas for improvements. He finally accepted the fact that I had some good ideas and encouraged me to write up in a proposal every month my one best idea so that he could get me the resources to tackle the solution on a formal basis. My first big project had to do with improving the inventory control in one of our manufacturing shops. Because the records for inventory receivable were inconsistent, I set up an entirely new inventory-order system and used that data to trace the history of the inventory—for example, when it was used, how it was used, and my recommendations for necessary replacement. I reduced the total value of the inventory we had to carry by 23 percent the first year. As a result, my supervisor would always use me as an example of someone who's constantly taking the initiative.

Describe a project you volunteered to work on to solve an existing problem or to avoid a potential problem. How did you approach your supervisor with the idea initially? Focus on the creativity of the idea, your approach, and the result you obtained.

Question 75: **Describe an improvement you personally initiated.**

Answer: I improved the inventory-management system for all laboratory supplies and equipment in a department of medicine at the university where I previously worked. The system was one that had been handed down year after year, and no one had ever bothered to question its efficiency. I decided we needed a whole new system, and I took it upon myself to design and implement one. This required several extra hours of work after my routine duties were completed, but I felt good about making this additional contribution to our department.

Give proof of your effectiveness, dedication to the job, and ability to "think outside of the box."

Question 76: **Describe a time in your work experience when the existing process didn't work and what you did about it.**

Answer: The order-entry system at the telecommunications company where I worked was a mess. Orders weren't being processed properly or in a timely manner. I did a work-flow analysis to identify the bottlenecks, and then I convinced my boss that we needed to spend one hundred thousand dollars on a totally new system. He reluctantly agreed, but with the caveat that "This had better save us money." After one year, the project had paid for the investment twofold.

The interviewer wants to know what initiatives this candidate took to change a faulty process in a creative way. Show that you can approach a problem creatively and manage a situation that isn't working. Did you achieve the result you needed?

Question 77: **Describe a time you had to alter your leadership style.**

Answer: I'm normally a strong leader who has good vision and enjoys delegating, but I expect my orders to be carried out promptly. When I was assigned a project to increase our product exports and was given a committee of nine people to work with, I immediately assumed I had the best plan and began my normal routine of delegating. I quickly realized, though, that this group of employees, with international backgrounds, wasn't responding well. In fact, they asked to have input into my plan. I agreed to spend half a day talking with them, and then I realized that they, too, had good ideas. The only way to move ahead on the project was to encourage the entire group to offer solutions to our export problem. I think these people would agree that I'm flexible and willing to modify my leadership style when the need arises.

Your answer to this question should emphasize your ability to make different kinds of people feel comfortable, so that a reasonable working relationship results. Be specific. What initiatives did you take to improve a less-than-ideal situation? What would the other people involved say about you now?

Question 78: **Tell me about a good process that you made even better.**

Answer: Recently, when I started a new job at a manufacturing company, the processes in place were very efficient and effective.

However, soon after beginning the job, I was told I'd have to reduce the budget by 20 percent. The only way to do this while maintaining the current workload was to make the processes even more efficient. I called my team together and issued a challenge that we had to take these already good processes and make them even better in order to meet the corporate objective. We exceeded even our own expectations and showed that any process can be improved, with critical evaluation and creative thinking.

The interviewer wants specific examples of how the candidate has added value, even when an existing situation was already good. In response to a question like this, prove you're creative enough to bring a new level of quality to the job. Can you demonstrate the value you've added in every past job?

Question 79: **Tell me about a time you persuaded others to adopt your idea.**

Answer: Our customer retention at the biotech company where I worked was poor. I thought we could understand and improve this situation by conducting a thorough customer-attitude survey. My boss thought this would be a waste of time, but I finally persuaded him that we could uncover some of the core reasons why retention had been getting progressively worse. I showed him how our competitors had been using customer surveys to their advantage. He agreed, and the surveys were used to make a number of changes in how we dealt with customers. For example, the survey revealed that customers were frustrated at not being able to quickly get through to the order-entry department—that the phone would often ring five or six times before someone would answer it. As one of the new supervisors, I started grabbing the phone on the first ring and helping to process the order. My initiative was noticed, and a few other supervisors started pitching in and doing the same thing. Before long, everyone was involved in answering the phone when we had an overload of incoming calls. This not only improved the efficiency of our order-entry process but caused all of the workers to take note that the supervisors truly were involved and interested in the department. Their efficiency also began to improve.

Emphasize here your ability to rally support and to make people comfortable with your ideas. Be specific. This question is common in interviews for sales positions.

Question 80: **How would a former colleague or subordinate describe your leadership style?**

Answer: My colleagues would probably say that my leadership style is the strong, silent type. I don't make a big deal about being in charge or making decisions. I try to involve everyone around me in the decision-making process and in carrying out a plan of action. My colleagues truly believe that I bring a lot of positive energy to our group and that I help motivate others.

The interviewer is trying to determine what the candidate's references or colleagues will say if they're called. Be objective and realistic without embellishing or being overly modest. Describe candidly your leadership style, giving specific examples that reflect your personal approach. Would former colleagues describe your contributions as generally positive for the department?

Question 81: **Do you believe that your job appraisals have adequately portrayed your leadership abilities?**

Answer: Although I had limited opportunity to demonstrate my leadership abilities in my previous job, I'm certain my appraisals would mention that I'm extremely thorough and dependable with my assignments. I take the time to make sure that all those around me clearly understand what our objectives are. This quality has enabled me to gain the confidence and respect of my coworkers and has been mentioned by my supervisor during performance appraisals.

This question is especially important if an outcome in your past work experience wasn't positive despite your efforts, or if you haven't had an opportunity to play a real leadership role.

Question 82:   **Describe the situations in which you're most comfortable as a leader.**

Answer: One of my talents is to take complex issues or problems and break them down into their simplest parts. I'm also good at teaching other people. As a result, whenever I'm faced with a complex problem, other people tend to let me find a solution and instruct them on how to proceed. As a result, I've found that I'm an effective leader in this kind of situation. I'm not a particularly effective leader, though, in a highly charged political environment. My preference is to deal with facts and data. When there are other issues like political or emotional factors to consider, I often prefer that someone else take the lead, and I simply resolve to be a good team player. In all other situations I normally surface as a leader.

Describe situations in which you've had experience as a creative leader and people have trusted you. Why do people tend to follow your lead in these situations? This is more an issue of earned authority than of outright authority. Conversely, if you're asked to describe situations in which you're a better contributor than leader, you can define types of problems that you're less comfortable working on or situations in which you feel you're too opinionated or biased to lead without controlling the group unfairly. Then end by describing instances when you've played the leader well.

Question 83:   **Describe your comfort level working with people of higher rank and people of lower rank.**

Answer: The person that delivers our mail twice a day has become a good friend. I've invited him to my house to meet my family, and we'll often go to baseball games together on the weekends. I can also relate well to my general manager. We both have common interests, which include sailing, and elk hunting in the winter.

Be specific here. Tell the interviewer how you've developed a style that's worked with a variety of people.

6. Compatibility with the Job

Question 84: **What were the most rewarding aspects of your most recent job?**

Answer: My favorite aspect of being a recruiter is the feeling of accomplishment you get when you know you've made a good match. I always make periodic checks on the recent recruits and their managers. Positive progress reports keep me motivated.

The interviewer is interested in how well suited the candidate is to the job. What do you do particularly well and want to do more of in your next position? Conclude by focusing on the new experiences you're seeking in your career. Your response should correspond closely to the position you're applying for.

Question 85: **What are the limitations of your current job?**

Answer: My job now is limited because the industry's simply not in a growth mode. Actually, that's why I became skilled in defensive marketing—retaining customers through customer-satisfaction programs that enhance our reputation and give us an edge over the competition.

Briefly explain one or two reasons why your current position doesn't allow for the growth you desire. Think about the question "Why are you ready to leave your current job?" Above all, remain positive, focusing on what you do well and want to emphasize in your work.

Question 86: **What do you want to achieve in your next job?**

Answer: I hope to be able to move into finance in a manufacturing group, since I started at the home office. I think that's important to my overall understanding of the company's core business.

Your answer should describe your ideal job. Focus on what you seek in your next job, taking care that your response closely matches the position you're applying for. Wherever you're unsure, ask questions of the interviewer—for example, "In this job would there be an opportunity to. . . ?"

Question 87: **Describe your ideal job.**

Answer: My ideal job would combine a sales territory that I managed and additional responsibility for sales training, so I could use my teaching background.

This question is similar to the previous one. Whatever response you prepare, make sure that it closely matches the position you're applying for.

Question 88: **What interests you most about this job?**

Answer: I was excited to watch your successful acquisitions in South America. Because of my exchange-program experience there, I believe I could help in your Latin American marketing effort.

Describe your qualifications for the job and how well the job fits your natural skills and abilities. Give evidence that you've performed well in similar work. What proof can you offer that you'll excel in this job?

Question 89: **What interests you least about this job?**

Answer: One of the things I hope not to do is prospect extensively by meeting one on one with small-account representatives. I found in my last sales territory that I gave superior service to my major accounts by focusing my on-site time with them. I was able to grow my key account business 20 percent.

You might want to ask the interviewer, "What did the last person in the job find difficult about the position?" Whatever the answer, respond appropriately, then describe what interests you most about the job.

Question 90: **What aspects of this job do you feel most confident about?**

Answer: I believe that I can engage an audience really effectively. When I get up in front of a room to present a new idea, I can usually get people on my side rather quickly.

Sell what you do best, and try to match it to the tasks you know are part of the job. Ask the interviewer if your skills might have been helpful in some recent project. Try to convince the interviewer that what you have to offer is truly in demand at the company, in this job, in the industry.

Question 91: **What concerns you most about performing this job?**

Answer: My clinical experience gives me confidence that I can perform the job. Other than the fact that I've not formally managed an outpatient clinic, I'm worried about whether the support staff is readily available to answer the phones. To get the results you want with your hot line, staff will have to be available at all times to answer questions about our services.

You may want to turn the question around; ask the interviewer if he or she has any concerns about your qualifications. Then address those concerns and affirm your confidence that your skills are the right ones and your interests are compatible with the position. Offer proof that will dispel any doubts the interviewer may have.

Question 92: **What skills do you offer that are most relevant to this job?**

Answer: My engineering background gives me a logical problem-solving ability that I know will be useful in assessing client needs. That background will also help your consulting firm sell business to manufacturers who themselves employ many engineers.

Your answer should be similar to your prepared response to the question "What interests you most about this job?" Use examples to back up the most relevant information from your resume.

Question 93: **Considering your own resume, what are your weaknesses in relation to this job?**

Answer: What are you most concerned about? If you're worried about my sincerity in working for a nonprofit organization, I hope that my discussion about my family's philanthropic efforts has made you more comfortable with my motives.

The best approach here is to turn the question around and get the interviewer to disclose what he or she believes are your weaknesses. Then use the opportunity to change the interviewer's mind. As always, give specific examples of your suitability for the position.

Question 94: **How did the realities differ from your expectations in your last job?**

Answer: The hardest thing to foresee was how other departments within the company would view my market-research department's work. Unfortunately, I found that many groups prefer to go outside for specialized research services, and that's really the reason I decided to contact your firm.

The interviewer is trying to determine if, in the past, the candidate was realistic about judging his or her suitability for a job. If, for the most part, you've been a pretty good judge of such things, you've probably screened yourself carefully for this job. The recruiter also wants to ensure that any past disenchantment won't be repeated in this job.

Question 95: **How would you enrich your current (or most recent) job?**

Answer: If I decide to stay with my current job, I'm going to volunteer to be on the communications task force, which is trying to get all of our offices linked to the Internet and other resources.

Without dwelling on the negatives, describe how you've improved the quality of your job so that you've continued to develop your skills and enjoy your work. Don't give the interviewer the impression that, if dissatisfied, you're unable to work on a solution or a plan for improvement. Conclude by focusing on the qualities you seek in your next job. Your response should correspond closely to the description of the position you're applying for.

Question 96: **Would you be able to travel as necessary to perform the job?**

Answer: If I have adequate notice, I can arrange to be available for travel at almost any time of the year. As it is, I usually travel about once a month for my current job.

Your response should be consistent with the demands of the position you're currently applying for, reflecting a realistic understanding of the work and time required. Inquire about seasonality of work, if you're unsure, and show a willingness to spend extended hours periodically.

Question 97: **Why is this a particularly good job for someone with your qualifications?**

Answer: Based on what you've told me about the last person who excelled in this job, I'm confident that I've the same skills in spreadsheet analysis and statistics. I'd also work well with your audit team, because I come from that kind of environment and know what a client can do to make the consulting relationship more productive.

The best answer here will describe positive experiences and results of recent jobs that were comparable to this one.

Question 98: **What's your most productive or ideal work setting?**

Answer: I like having at least one hour of uninterrupted time in the early morning to plan my day. I usually start around 7 A.M. Otherwise, I enjoy an office with open doors, constant feedback, and lots of energy and activity. It helps me work more productively when I sense how busy everyone else is, too.

The interviewer wants to know the impact that the candidate's working environment has on his or her job performance. How well would you fit the position, physical layout of the department, and attitudes of the particular work group? Emphasize your ability to work in a variety of settings and how you've managed to be productive in less-than-ideal work environments.

Question 99: **Do you prefer continuity in structure or frequent change in your daily work?**

Answer: I enjoy change and challenge, which is why I frequently ask for the tough assignments. The last two projects we discussed were ones that I asked for. I don't allow myself to get bored.

Your answer should be consistent with the job description. Describe environments that have allowed you to remain interested and learn new things without getting bored.

7. Personality and Cultural Compatibility

Question 100: **What would your friends tell me about you?**

Answer: My friends would tell you that I move faster than most people, eat more than most people, work later than most people, and still manage to spend time with friends despite my schedule. I believe in doing lots of things with gusto.

Talk about parts of your personality that will naturally be revealed on the job.

Question 101: **Tell me about your relationship with your previous bosses.**

Answer: My bosses would tell you that I've often acted as a sounding board for them. With all three of my bosses, we've mentored each other, although the obvious balance of wisdom and expertise was theirs. I was always helpful to them in their decisions about customer problems.

The interviewer is interested in whether the candidate and the supervisor for the position will work well together. As you describe each previous boss, the interviewer will most likely be making mental comparisons to the supervisor. The interviewer must feel confident that he or she has uncovered any surprises about your working relationships, and that you won't end up clashing with your new boss. Try to be honest without being negative. Emphasize the type of boss you work well with.

Question 102: **Describe your working relationship with your colleagues.**

Answer: They'd probably tell you that nothing ever shocks me or sets me back too much, and that I'm really an asset as an adviser when they suffer a roadblock, as in the case we discussed about the contractor. I'm constant and dependable.

What types of people do you enjoy working with? How would the company's customers or clients react to you? From your answer the interviewer must feel confident that any surprises about your work personality have been uncovered. Give examples of how you pitched in, how you know to ask for help when you need it, and your concern for the group's accomplishments.

Question 103: **Describe your personality beneath the professional image.**

Answer: I laugh a lot at my own shortcomings. I see irony in most things and I'm outspoken, but I bring a sense of humor to any office. I think it provides a nice balance of warmth in a work setting.

This is similar to the question "What would your friends tell me about you?" Concentrate on how your personality reflects your job skills or interests.

Question 104: **What environments allow you to be especially effective?**

Answer: Although I can work effectively in most environments, I prefer environments where people are their own bosses, within reason. I like to have a goal but be able to draw my own map to get there. To accomplish goals, I rely on asking questions and finding people receptive, so cooperation and access are important to me in a work group.

Emphasize your flexibility and your ability to work in many different types of environments. Your answer should not consist of a laundry list of requirements (private office, few interruptions, and so on) or the interviewer may conclude that you will be difficult to satisfy.

Question 105: **Describe an environment that is ineffective for you.**

Answer: I don't do terribly well when someone has an exact idea of how one of my goals should be accomplished. That doesn't allow me any latitude to make adjustments to suit my own style. I do well when I can draw my own map.

This is the negative side of "What environments allow you to be especially effective?" Focus on environments you prefer or that increase your effectiveness.

Question 106: **What situations excite and motivate you?**

Answer: I really enjoy working on any re-engineering project where a true improvement results—for example, the JIT project in which we saved more than ten thousand dollars per month in inventory costs.

The interviewer wants a clearer perspective as to what kind of work inspires you. There is no one right answer to this question, but your answer should be at least somewhat compatible with the position you're applying for. For example, you should not say that highly creative work motivates you if you're applying for a position that involves somewhat monotonous, repetitive work, such as data entry or assembly-line work.

Question 107: **How would your last employer describe your work habits and ethics?**

Answer: Let me put it this way: I received an MVP award from my division for the extra efforts I put into one of our customer relationships. The customer had threatened to pull the account, so I stepped in and debugged the system, even though it required me to work through a holiday weekend.

Do you think your current or last employer would hire you again? Are you reliable, thorough, dependable? Give examples of your reliability, dedication, and corporate loyalty.

Question 108: **How do you feel your company treats its employees?**

Answer: In recent years, management has really been dedicated to having a satisfied workforce. Their efforts, however, often rekindle past upheavals, when employees made sacrifices for the company and received little in return. In human resources we spend a lot of money trying to break down the walls between exempt and nonexempt employees. If "the company" is management, I would have to say management is making a conscious effort to mend fences and to do right by our employees.

The interviewer wants to see if you can walk the fine line between loyalty to management and concern for the employees. Although there's no right answer to this question, you should try to avoid bias and to comment as objectively as possible on your company's attitude and approach toward employees. Be prepared to give examples that reflect your company's view toward its employees.

Question 109: **Did your customers or clients enjoy working with you?**

Answer: My client base changed very little, except that billings increased, so I think that's evidence the clients were satisfied enough to stay with me for more than three years. That's particularly unusual in the ad-agency business, too. They simply knew they could count on me to treat their business as if it were my own.

How would the company's customers or clients react to you? Can you give specific feedback from a client? How many of your clients were repeat customers? Why do you believe you kept their business?

Question 110: **How will you complement this department?**

Answer: I enjoy an environment in which people bounce ideas off each other and have the flexibility to ask for help when they need it. I'm usually a great troubleshooter for PC problems in my office, and I'm often going to ask for help proofreading important memos. I believe in give-and-take.

Describe how your personality and/or skills would help round out the department. What types of people enjoy working with you for hours at a time? How would the company's customers or clients react? Assure the interviewer that there will be no surprises about your work personality.

Question 111: **Whom did you choose as your references, and why?**

Answer: I selected a former boss, a peer, and a customer as references, to demonstrate that I'm a pretty well-rounded person and get along with all the important work associates in my life.

The interviewer is looking for a logical mix of people without any obvious omissions. For example, a former salesperson would do well to include a former salesperson as a reference. Describe what you'd expect each of your references to say. Include a diverse group—senior to junior, an associate from work, an old professor from college.

Question 112: **Can we call all of your references?**

Answer: I'd prefer that you call my current boss only after you've made me a firm offer of employment and I've had a chance to tell her myself that I'm changing jobs. Then, of course, I understand your need to verify that my application was accurate.

This is a question designed to protect you. If your current employer doesn't know you're looking for a new job (as is most often the case), you can request that the interviewer contact your current employer only after you've accepted a position and given your notice to your current employer.

Question 113: **Tell me what you learned from a recent book.**

Answer: I enjoy reading biographies, especially of people who lived in a different era. I recently read Churchill's biography, which taught me a lot about the value of leadership and good PR under times of stress.

The interviewer wants to know if the candidate has interests in common with others at the company. Do you use your spare time as a productive, yet relaxing, way to learn new things? What are you naturally inquisitive about?

Question 114: **Tell me about a work group you really enjoyed.**

Answer: My group in our new-product-launch department really meshed. When one of us was approaching the final day before a launch, we all rolled up our sleeves and helped put press packets together or whatever else was the last item to be shipped to the sales force. Although it was an administrative task, it had to be done, and it was a good time for us all to speculate on the success of the product and any major concerns.

This question is a combination of "Describe your working relationship with your colleagues," and "Did your customers or clients enjoy working with you?" Demonstrate your ability to work well with others and to establish solid, ongoing working relationships.

Question 115: **Describe a time when you had to assist a coworker.**

Answer: I once helped an associate understand survey method-ology in order to write a report. He had never taken a research course and didn't know how to structure questions.

Demonstrate a willingness to pitch in. Discuss a time when your objective advice or special expertise produced a positive outcome for a coworker and for the department.

Question 116: **Are you most productive working alone or in a group?**

Answer: I need some private time for planning, but otherwise I like the activity and noise of people around me and the ability to share ideas. I think most writers need reinforcement, because we all get writer's block occasionally.

The interviewer is looking for someone who can work in an environment without the environment disrupting the candidate's preferred way of getting work done. Be honest but communicate that you're a flexible and reasonably adaptable employee.

Question 117: **Tell me about a situation in which it was difficult to remain objective.**

Answer: I'd researched a new on-line source for our library, and my manager decided to pull funding at the last minute. It was frus-trating for me because I'd gotten excited about the product, liked the vendor, and had even told some people to count on having the resource. But I understand the need to revise budgets, and the matter was out of my control at the time.

The obvious example here is a time when you've worked long hours on a project only to have the project canceled. Or perhaps you found that the project was less strategically sound than you'd hoped.

Were you able to readjust your thinking and do what was best in the long run?

8. Management Style and Interpersonal Skills

Question 118: **Tell me about an effective manager, supervisor, or other person in a leading role you've known.**

Answer: The best professor I ever had always reviewed the most important points from our last class before he moved on to new material. He also watched our faces carefully and repeated information whenever he saw a blank stare. Sometimes he would just ask for feedback by saying, "What are you having difficulty with?" He never assumed too much or made us feel dumb for not grasping a concept quickly.

Talk about a supervisor's management style and interpersonal skills. Focus on the positive—how the person worked rather than what type of work he or she did. How was the person able to accomplish so much and get your support?

Question 119: **What type of management style do you think is effective?**

Answer: I've always learned well from people who act as coaches rather than experts. When someone comes to me with a problem, I try to act as if I'm reasoning through the problem with the person, learning as I go. I never just give an answer. I want employees to develop confidence in creating answers for themselves.

This is similar to the question "Tell me about an effective manager or supervisor you've known." Give a personal or popular example of a leader you believe is effective. Why is this person able to accomplish so much? Talk about your management style and inter-personal skills with peer groups and leaders, and describe how you've incorporated habits from leaders you admire.

Question 120: **Describe your personal management style.**

Answer: I repeat what someone has told me, but I reorganize the information in a way that helps them see the problem or answer themselves. Sometimes I just ask questions until they see a clear solution. I learned this from watching a friend who's a successful trial lawyer.

Talk about your management style and interpersonal skills with peer groups and leaders, and describe how you've incorporated a habit from a leader you admire.

Question 121: **What type of people do you work with most effectively?**

Answer: I tend to work well with people who are confident and straightforward. It's more difficult for me to be around timid people, because I move quickly and am decisive.

Focus on the positive here. What type of boss, employee, and colleague would you be? Keep in mind that the interviewer wants to find out how well you would fit in with the other personalities in the company—not how well the other personalities in the company would suit you.

Question 122: **What things impress you in colleagues?**

Answer: I admire and work best with people who are of good character and have integrity. I also think confidence and enthusiasm is positive in any business environment.

The recruiter will want to see how developed your interpersonal skills are. More than likely, you'll be interacting not only with your own department, but with other people in the company, and possibly colleagues. Show the recruiter that you will shine in this area.

Question 123: **What are some of the things your supervisor did that you disliked?**

Answer: The only thing I really don't like is to get feedback in front of others. I want to hear good or bad feedback in private, so that I have time to think and react to the issue without other distractions. I believe that's the fair way to improve learning or to change future behavior.

Try to describe a positive learning experience from a difficult situation, avoiding personal criticism of an ex-boss or manager, if possible.

Question 124: **How do you organize and plan for major projects?**

Answer: I love to brainstorm a best, worst, and most likely scenario. Then I set a timetable that's realistic. What I usually find is that some combination of my best and worst cases evolves; I can adjust my schedule easily as these things unfold because I've already visualized what could happen and how I'd react.

Give the interviewer a good idea of your general approach to mastering complex tasks. You may wish to include here how you decide on time frames, set deadlines, determine priorities, delegate tasks, and decide what to do for yourself.

Question 125: **Describe a time when you've worked under intense pressure.**

Answer: I had to complete an end-of-quarter report once while I was on the road for two consecutive weeks. The amount of telephoning back and forth was incredible, because I couldn't bring my office files with me. Luckily I had a great secretary and a logical filing system, so we located everything we needed.

A good idea when answering a question like this is to concentrate on your time-management skills. Give a specific example, with enough detail to communicate both the intensity of the situation and the ease with which you handled it.

Question 126: **How do you manage your time on a typical day?**

Answer: I've always given priority to work with established clients, because they offer a better risk/return value. The last thing I do is general correspondence, especially internal correspondence, which I take care of at the end of the day or week.

Here the interviewer wants evidence that the candidate can juggle priorities as necessary based on the work team, departmental adjustments, and nature of the tasks. He or she will also want to be sure that you don't give priority to fun work and avoid dull, necessary routines that are important in the long run.

Question 127: **Describe a time when you acted on someone's suggestion.**

Answer: I changed my open office hours because several of my employees found it difficult to visit me except in the early mornings.

Be specific here in demonstrating your flexibility and your interpersonal skills. Do people feel comfortable offering you suggestions? Do they believe you'll listen fairly and objectively? When you do take their advice, do you give credit where credit is due? Reassure the interviewer that your approach to management is reasonable and fair, and that you respect other people's good ideas.

Question 128: **Tell me about a time when you had to defend an idea to your boss.**

Answer: Once I had to convince my boss to change PR firms. I really believed that our interests on the West Coast weren't being met by our Chicago-based firm. I was able to convince him after showing him the demographic shift in our customer base.

This is the flip side of "Describe a time when you acted on someone's suggestion." Can you give advice constructively and get someone to understand your side? Give a specific example.

Question 129: **What aspect of your management style would you like to change?**

Answer: I've been working on holding back the urge to tell people the answers when they ask for advice. I think it's more important to teach people how to solve their own problems. I've gotten better at coaching and presenting questions and feedback without telling people what to do.

Talk about one aspect of your management style that you're working to improve. Tell the interviewer the steps you're taking and give evidence that you're making progress.

Question 130: **Have you ever felt defensive around your boss or peers?**

Answer: I had to explain once why I thought a black-and-white brochure was more suitable for the content of an insurance-product brochure. No one in my office liked the idea initially, because we were all used to color brochures, and everybody felt that black and white looked cheap. Eventually I convinced them that a more subtle approach would work better to present information about a difficult topic—death benefits.

Pick a specific example of a time when you had to defend an idea. Avoid any discussion of personality clashes, feelings of resentment, or heated exchanges. How did you get others to see your view of things? What was the outcome? Be sure to end on a positive note.

Question 131: **Tell me about a learning experience that affected your management style.**

Answer: Early in my job at the bank, I wrote an e-mail to an EVP but failed to copy the two AVPs who worked for him. One of them was impacted by the content of the memo and concluded that I'd circumvented him on purpose. I've really been careful about chain of command ever since.

Use a variation of your answer to the question "Tell me about your least-favorite manager or supervisor," in which you describe an experience, either positive or negative, that taught you a lesson about effective management. Or describe the tactics of a manager who got you to perform more than you thought was possible. How did he or she motivate you?

Question 132: **Have you patterned your management style after someone in particular?**

Answer: I've emulated my first boss in many ways. I keep a folder for each member of my staff on the company intranet site. They can throw e-mails, ideas, work they want me to review, or anything else in there, and I do the same with material I have for them. It's an extra form of communication whenever one of us gets an idea. Then, when we sit down to talk, the issues we need to cover are in one place, at our fingertips.

Your answer should describe someone you've known person-ally—a boss who motivated you in a positive way to achieve beyond your own goals. Be specific about how he or she accomplished this.

Question 133: **Describe a leader you admire.**

Answer: I've always admired the president of my company. He's visible, he doesn't want a special parking place or table in the cafeteria, and he gives you the feeling that he's just another member of the team.

Give personal or popular examples of leaders you believe are effective. Why do you believe those people are able to accomplish so much? What tricks have you learned from the leaders you admire?

Question 134: **What personal characteristics add to your effectiveness?**

Answer: I always stay in touch with my network. If I see an article that might be of interest to someone I know, I send a PDF to that person. Then, when I need help and make a phone call to that person, the phone call gets returned promptly.

Talk about what makes your personal style unique and effective. For example, how are you able to get cooperation from others? What specific skills and traits help you get results, and why?

9. Problem-Solving Ability

Question 135: **How have your technical skills been an asset?**

Answer: Although I never planned on a career as a writer or publisher, much of my job in marketing has depended on good writing and creative layout skills. My part-time college job with a newspaper taught me a lot about desktop publishing, how to position something on a page effectively, and how to write short sentences with maximum impact. In all of my marketing jobs, I've been able to explain my goals clearly to graphic designers, which has helped me avoid costly design revisions.

Describe how you've used technical skills to solve a problem. Tell a specific story. Demonstrate how these same skills have been useful in other situations or in most of the jobs you've held. If you're hired, what situations will you handle particularly well?

Question 136: **Describe a situation in which you've applied technical skills to solve a problem.**

Answer: One of our components kept arriving at distribution points with stress cracks. My materials-science background helped me to diagnose the problem as one of storage temperature during shipping. Although our equipment was safely stored at both end points, it had been sitting in un-air-conditioned cargo space for up to thirty hours before reaching its destination. We're now using a different shipping company, and we've improved our labeling on large shipments to reflect the user's warning about temperature extremes.

Quickly define the problem for the interviewer, then focus on how your skills enabled you to tackle it. What actions did you take, and what was the outcome?

Question 137: **How do your technical skills, combined with other skills, add to your effectiveness on the job?**

Answer: My strong economics background, along with my computer-sales experience, provide a balanced set of skills to perform financial research on the computer industry. Most of my contacts and hobbies are also related to high tech, so I offer a natural curiosity that helps me stay abreast of changes in the industry.

This question gives you a chance to sell the package deal—why is the unique combination of your skills effective? Give one or two specific examples of projects you're frequently asked to handle.

Question 138: **Describe how you've used a problem-solving process.**

Answer: We once had several customers who'd arranged numerous free hotel stays around the country using our 100 percent satisfaction guarantee. I suggested leading a PC task force to set up a warning system that flags any guest name corresponding to a previous reported complaint or free service. Now when a guest checks in and we type in a name, we know immediately that the person has had an unpleasant experience at one of our hotels. We proactively approach the guest, acknowledge we're aware of the problem, and offer our commitment to do everything possible to provide them with impeccable service. This practice warns the potentially fraudulent guest; at the same time, it warns our staff to be especially careful with any guest who's giving our hotel a second chance. Our satisfaction rate has improved, and fraudulent cases have decreased.

Describe for the interviewer, step by step, how a problem-solving process you initiated came to a successful conclusion. What measures or benchmarks did you use to control or manage the process? What were the results?

Question 139: **How do you usually go about solving a problem?**

Answer: When I need to solve a problem, I generally start by writing down as many ideas as I can think of about possible causes. Next I look for relationships among causes so I can group together symptoms of bigger problems. Usually, after I study these groups of problems, the real cause becomes readily apparent.

The interviewer will want to hear the logic you use to solve problems as well as the outcomes you're able to achieve. Are you decisive? How do you narrow the options and make decisions? What do people say about your reasoning skills? What examples would they cite of your effective decision making?

Question 140: **How do you measure the success of your work?**

Answer: I measure reactions of customers. When my customers call me with a referral, I know they're happy. And I have to say that repeat business to me is more satisfying than winning a new account. People have a tendency to try a new company because of that company's reputation or product, but they come back because of the relationship they've learned to trust.

What results or evidence do you need to evaluate the success of your work? What type of feedback or reward system is important to you? The reviewer will want to establish that these needs can be satisfied in the job.

Question 141: **How practical or pragmatic are you?**

Answer: I can usually pick up on an underlying problem, even if it's not too obvious. I recall an investment banker who visited our real-estate-finance class and asked us what might cause the Tokyo investment community a problem in attracting local investment dollars. A number of finance M.B.A.'s in the class started trying to think of some complicated set of reasons. I decided it would have to do with getting out of a bad market quickly, and that a nonliquid investment would create problems. I said investors would be unsettled if the primary investment is local real estate and inflation has caused the paper value to exaggerate the real street value. As it ended up, that was the answer he wanted.

Give the interviewer an example of some practical or sensible approach you've used to solve a problem. When was a simple solution the best solution? Had others overlooked the obvious? In this example, you'll want to show off your commonsense skills rather than your academic skills.

Question 142: **How do you balance your reliance on facts with your reliance on intuition?**

Answer: Facts are important but often neglect point-in-time influences, especially with market research. One survey that I was uncomfortable with involved pricing data that was collected just after a major presidential election. The timing caused me to doubt that consumers would really spend as much as the survey indicated they would for new cars. So we ended up holding on to the last quarter's pricing structure. We sold more cars while, as interest rates climbed, some of our competitors had expensive inventory carryover.

Describe a specific time when your intuition helped you solve a problem that might have been handled badly if you'd followed the facts or standard procedure. Demonstrate an ability to "think outside of the box."

Question 143: **What was your greatest problem in your last job?**

Answer: I had to get longtime employees with few or no computer skills to embrace a new e-mail system. I started by explaining the need for less paper in everyone's job. Then I decided to create a temporary e-mail account with one daily riddle on the system; everyone who responded correctly got their name put in a weekly drawing. Each week for one month a person from the drawing got dinner for four at a nice local restaurant. This approach went over well as a device to get people to use the system.

The interviewer wants to hear about a problem area the candidate improved in his or her last job. If you're asked this question, don't complain without showing solutions. Demonstrate an ability to offer solutions, not merely to point out problems.

Question 144: **Tell me about a problem that you failed to anticipate.**

Answer: My boss asked me to solve an ongoing scheduling problem. I failed to realize that the person who had lived with the problem would see me as an antagonist. By the time I realized it, I'd already done some of the groundwork. If I'd started by asking for the person's opinion, I would have been able to get him on my side early on.

This question forces you to be humble but gives you an opportunity to relate an incident from which you learned an important lesson. What warning signs should you have seen? How has your judgment improved as a result of this experience?

Question 145: **Have you ever resolved a long-standing problem?**

Answer: We used to batch our guests' personal faxes—sometimes as many as ten outgoing fax requests per hour—to put less strain on our administrative staff. We had guests who weren't happy about that. I arranged a lease deal on an outgoing fax machine for guest self-serve access. This freed up more time for staff, and they were able to maintain control of incoming faxes, protecting incoming information until they could locate the appropriate guest in person.

Tell the interviewer about a problem you championed within a work setting or other organization. How did you overcome or circumvent the obstacles? What were the results? What motivated you to tackle the problem to begin with?

Question 146: **Describe a time you found it necessary to make an unpopular decision.**

Answer: I had to start a policy of no food in work areas, including private offices, because the production workers were unhappy with the inequity. For safety reasons workers couldn't have food anywhere near expensive equipment. Now it's forgotten, but at the time a number of supervisors were angry at me. I thought the matter was important and that the solution was consistent with other new policies, like doing away with assigned parking spaces for high-level employees. So far we've been progressive enough to keep unions out of our company.

Sometimes an important long-term result is achieved only with short-term sacrifices. This question measures the candidate's ability to make important value judgments with long-term results. Be sure to give a specific example if you're asked a question like this.

Question 147: **Tell me about the most difficult problem you've ever dealt with.**

Answer: I was promoted to manage a new department. A coworker in that group resented me from the beginning. I soon learned that her best friend had been turned down for the position. I actually confronted her about it; I explained that I had once put a friendship to the test because I'd worked too closely with someone and we found that we spent our leisure time talking about work. A few weeks after our talk, she admitted that she'd never thought about the potential results of working too closely with a personal friend. Our working relationship was fine after that.

Discuss the problem here briefly, then focus on what actions you took and what results you obtained. Be candid—why was this problem personally hard for you? How did you remain objective and professional?

Question 148: **Describe a time when a problem wasn't resolved to your satisfaction.**

Answer: I thought once that we'd let a customer down by not responding quickly enough to resolve a problem; our production capacity wasn't sufficient to deliver the customer's complete order during the holiday season. That customer ended up asking for a discount, and I thought we should have offered the discount first, without waiting to be asked. The sense of goodwill would have been stronger.

This question focuses on the candidate's standards of quality. Describe a situation in which you foresaw long-term complications from a problem that was poorly handled. Did you do anything to try to resolve the issue?

Question 149: **Tell me about a time when there was no rule or precedent to help you attack a problem.**

Answer: I was the first employee in a newly created position. I spent the first week developing an understanding of the history that had led to creation of the position. Only then did a method for setting priorities on the job become clear.

Can you operate without structure? Describe your problem-solving process, especially the steps you took and measures you established in a particularly trying situation. Demonstrate confidence and the willingness to take on new challenges.

Question 150: **When do you have difficulty making choices?**

Answer: I'm not particularly good at interpreting survey data. I've really worked to get to know our research staff and librarians. I rely on them and am careful to thank them formally in front of my vice president. We're definitely a team, and I'm careful not to take credit for our industry reports, which we publish for the Pacific region of our firm.

Be honest. What situations are difficult for you to resolve? What people, or other resources, do you gather in these instances to help you make decisions?

Question 151: **Describe an opportunity in which you felt the risks far outweighed the rewards.**

Answer: At one point we had an opportunity to purchase conveyor equipment at thirty cents on the dollar from a company that had dissolved. Although we anticipated an overhaul of our distribution facility five years down the road, I felt it was too far into the future to spend money only to have idle capacity for a five-year period. If market conditions had shown more promise for new sales in the initial two-year period, I would have gone ahead with it.

The interviewer wants to see that the candidate has an interest in taking reasonable risks without inclining toward foolishness. Demonstrate with an example your logic for deciding against some plan. How was the outcome preferable to what might have happened?

10. Accomplishments

Question 152: **Tell me about a major accomplishment.**

Answer: I'm really proud of the business I obtained with XYZ Wholesale Club. I believe that these types of companies will continue to thrive in the next few years.

Offer proof of your accomplishments using real examples. Don't give long descriptions of situations. Focus your answer on the actions you took and the positive results you obtained. The interviewer will want to know what you can contribute to the company.

Question 153: **Talk about a contribution you've made to a team.**

Answer: I helped my last team put together more cohesive presentations for a client. I think our practice and preparation made a statement about how committed we would be to the details of the system installation. In the end, we landed the account.

Tell the interviewer about your initiative within a team. Offer proof, using specific examples, that you delivered more than the team expected and that the team would compliment your contributions to the group's efforts. What special role did you play?

Question 154: **Talk about a special contribution you've made to an employer.**

Answer: In my last job I ran the United Way campaign for three consecutive years. I believe it's an important cause, and I know it's difficult for the company to find volunteers, so I stepped in.

Let the interviewer know that you deliver more than your employer expects. If you were hired, what situations would you handle especially well? What unique contributions can you make to the organization? How would you go the extra mile?

Question 155: **Tell me about an organization outside of work that's benefited from your participation.**

Answer: I've been involved in Junior Achievement. I was an economics undergrad, and I liked seeing the high-school kids get excited about what they read in the paper and about how economics affects their lives.

Discuss in some detail your initiative with something you volunteered for—such as working for a charitable organization. In other words, what things are important motivators for you? Could your employer benefit from these interests in some way? What kind of corporate citizen are you?

Question 156: **Give me an example of a time you delivered more than was expected.**

Answer: In my last job my boss asked me to take over all the uncollected accounts. I was able to recover 20 percent more than his goal. I convinced people that I was willing to work out an affordable schedule based on their needs, and I did this by asking about their problems. Once they vented, they would usually listen to me.

Give an example of a time when you truly excelled at a given task. Chances are you're likely to repeat similar results in your new position. In other words, give the interviewer an indication of the situations you might handle especially well if you were hired.

Question 157: **What accomplishment is your greatest source of pride?**

Answer: I'm proud of how we turned a profit at our hospital in the first year under private management. Now that goal's been accomplished, and I'm ready to do the same for another hospital; that's why consulting within the industry appeals to me so much.

Your answer will hint at the kinds of projects you'd like to do in the future. Focus on goals related specifically to the job you're applying for. The interviewer will want to know how your past initiative and accomplishments can translate to success for his or her company.

Question 158:   **If I hired you today, what would you accomplish first?**

Answer: I could help you increase your business within the OEM market. As an OEM contractor for four years, I understand how to structure deals that will be profitable.

Give the interviewer clear, tangible evidence that the company will benefit immediately upon hiring you. Focus your answer on the action you would take, and make sure your goals are realistic. Can you demonstrate specific knowledge about the company and industry and how it relates to the role of your department and job?

Question 159:   **What accomplishment was the most difficult for you to achieve?**

Answer: I found it intimidating to work with the marketing-research staff when I started my job, mostly because I hadn't done well in statistics or market research during college. What I decided to do was enroll in an executive seminar on market research, which really boosted my confidence. Now I don't feel at a disadvantage when I meet with the research group, and I know what questions to ask to get information that's meaningful to me.

Describe something you've accomplished despite obstacles, lack of training, or inadequate experience. This question allows you to talk about overcoming a weakness.

Question 160:   **Tell me about a time you saved money for an employer or an organization.**

Answer: I was able to eliminate a middleman we'd worked with for years in getting our employee magazine printed. We planned the issues, collected research, wrote the articles, did most of the editing, and then handed the information to him, which he took to a designer and printer. After I managed this process twice, I decided to do the coordinating work myself. The additional time it cost me was eight hours, but we saved a 10 percent markup, and even better, the issues now get completed faster and with greater accuracy.

Be specific and quantify your results when answering your question, but don't give long descriptions of situations. Offer proof using a clear, convincing example.

Question 161: **What's your greatest achievement to date?**

Answer: I'm proud of the fact that I graduated on time with a solid GPA while I played varsity basketball for four years. A lot of the women on my team either took a reduced course load or let their grades suffer. I believe the reason I got through it all was sheer determination; I never even let myself visualize anything but finishing on time and with good grades. So I firmly believe, as a professional counselor, in the importance of a positive outlook.

Be sure that the achievement you describe here is relevant to the job you're interviewing for. Also, be careful that your answer doesn't sound as if the best is behind you. Mention something great that you've achieved, but clearly communicate your belief that the best is yet to come.

Question 162: **Tell me about a person or group you had to work with to achieve something important.**

Answer: My law-school class really worked hard to improve the image of our school with employers. We put together our own promotional book, which we sent to law firms and alumni. The book presented a mock courtroom case in which other law schools filed a class-action suit arguing that the quality of the student body and teaching at our school had caused an erosion of interest in other law programs; they proved to the court that both teaching and student statistics clearly had led to positive placements for our graduates, which in turn killed the chances for students from other programs. The format of our brochure was so unusual that it got the attention of the major press, which served our purpose nicely.

Give an example that demonstrates your use of teamwork to produce a better result than you could have achieved by yourself. Acknowledge your contributions and those of your team members.

Question 163:   **Tell me about something you accomplished that required discipline.**

Answer: I had to work two jobs to put myself through graduate school. I interned at the newspaper while I studied journalism during the week. Then on weekends, I sold real estate. Juggling those three schedules was a challenge, but I did it because it was important to me to graduate without school loans.

This is your opportunity to discuss a skill you worked to develop, or a time when the quantity of your work required solid time-management skills. How did you remain focused?

Question 164:   **What situations do your colleagues rely on you to handle?**

Answer: People often rely on me to handle client confrontations. I'm known as a person who never loses my temper in front of customers.

This question provides a good opportunity for the candidate to showcase his or her dependability, strength of character, and professionalism. The interviewer will be impressed if you can also demonstrate that you work well with others and clearly enjoy your colleagues' respect.

Question 165:   **Tell me about a need you fulfilled within a group or a committee.**

Answer: I worked on the committee to review our company's policy on sick leave. One of our employees was abusing the system in order to gain vacation time. I served as the objective member of the group, having used virtually no sick leave in five years of employment. I ended up presenting an idea that the company's now considering, which is to allow up to one week of sick time to be voluntarily allocated to extra family-leave time.

Tell the interviewer about your initiative in group projects. In teams, what roles do you usually play?

Question 166: **Tell me how you've supported and helped attain a corporate goal.**

Answer: I helped meet our goal of value to stockholders by holding a fire sale of goods to clean out our warehouse. The public was invited, with a preview for customers, suppliers, vendors, and stockholders. Attendees bought new but visually imperfect electronics components at 70 percent reductions. We cleared twenty thousand dollars from sales of equipment we'd written off.

Here the interviewer asks for evidence that the candidate completes projects with the corporation's goals in mind. What other groups, departments, or customers benefited from a similar effort on your part? Give specific examples, not generalizations. Focus on how you've enriched your job by expanding the benefits of your action beyond your own group or department.

Question 167: **Tell me about a quantifiable outcome of one of your efforts.**

Answer: I reorganized inventory planning and was able to automate the inventory-reorder function, which used to be a forty-hour process and now takes only three hours.

Describe a specific accomplishment, the outcome of which produced a clear benefit. Offer proof, using real examples, that you deliver more than what's expected. Did you exceed your expected outcome? How?

Question 168: **Describe an ongoing problem you were able to overcome.**

Answer: We had three groups with different homegrown schedules, even though each group relied on the others' work and timing. I got us all connected via a computer network and held a training session to brainstorm our communications plan. We now talk regularly via e-mail and a network scheduler, and we all have the information we need.

This question is similar to "Tell me about a time you tackled an unpopular assignment." Focus on how you achieved good results through the use of a creative technique or through greater diligence than others had previously devoted to the project.

Question 169: **Tell me about a project you completed ahead of schedule.**

Answer: I was in charge of a new product rollout. In general we completed each phase without a major setback—which was partially luck—but I also systematically called two days ahead of every deadline to check the status with all groups involved. I believe that made the difference. The launch took place two weeks ahead of plan—a significant period of time in our industry, where shelf life for products is generally less than one year.

Focus here on how you set goals and schedules, measured results, and championed the outcome of a project. This question is aimed at your diligence in accomplishing tasks and, assuming the project required group effort, at your leadership skills.

11. Career Aspirations

Question 170: **Where do you hope that your career will have progressed to in the next few years?**

Answer: Over the next few years I'd like to have progressed to the point where I have bottom-line budget responsibility, and I'm also in charge of a production unit where I have labor-relations, quality-control, design, and manufacturing responsibilities. I believe this job will go a long way to helping me meet my career goals.

Avoid the temptation to suggest job titles; this makes you seem unbending and unrealistic, since you don't know or control the system of promotion. Likewise, you don't know how long it might have taken your interviewer to reach certain levels, and you wouldn't want to insult. Describe new experiences or responsibilities you'd like to add that build on the job you're applying for.

Question 171: **What are your long-term career plans?**

Answer: My long-term career goals are to become known as an industry expert and to have earned a respectable management position with responsibility for a major piece of the business. I'd like to think I'll have experience in many parts of the business over time.

It's reasonable to see ahead about five years but probably no more, given the changing nature of businesses. Especially in high-tech fields, which change dramatically in a short time, it's impossible to project accurately how you might fit into a specific job. Therefore, focus on types of experiences (not job titles) you hope to gain over time.

Question 172: **Since this will be your first job, how do you know you'll like the career path?**

Answer: Although it's true that I've never worked a job in your industry, I've talked to many friends and alums at my school who've been successful in your company. I always ask them the questions, "What's the most frustrating thing about your job?" and "What's the most rewarding thing about your job?" From the information I've gained, I'm confident that I'll be able to adapt quickly to your culture and will find the next few years rewarding, based on my goals and values.

This can be a difficult question to answer convincingly, unless you've done a little bit of preparation. Discuss, for example, an internship or a conversation that's allowed you to assess the culture of the organization or to preview the work involved. Describe other people in the profession who have been mentors or who have taught you about the field. Also, point out why you're interested, how you learned more about the industry, and how you stay current with industry trends.

Question 173: **Why is this job right for you at this time in your career?**

Answer: This job would build on my extensive technical background both as a navy communications officer and in the two software companies where I've worked. I believe I'm now ready to assume broader responsibilities as a project manager. I've demonstrated my ability to handle the responsibility for both a diverse team of programmers and engineers and for major capital budgets.

Describe the experiences you want to pursue that build on your current skills and interests. Be as specific as you can, based on what you know about the current or future direction of the position and the department. Demonstrate why this position fits with your personal career goals. How can you create job growth for yourself?

Question 174: **What are your aspirations beyond this job?**

Answer: Beyond this job as a marketing assistant, I see myself moving up through marketing analysis into brand management and eventually running a category. I'm aware that there are several skills I need to develop in the interval, and I believe with your continuing-education program and my own motivation for self-improvement, I'll have those skills when the opportunities arise for greater responsibility. That's why I'm determined to learn from the ground up, starting as a marketing assistant.

Again, don't fall into the trap of specifying job titles. Stick to a natural progression you see as plausible. How should this job grow for the good of the organization? Then turn your attention once again to the job at hand. If you seem too interested in what lies beyond this job, the interviewer will fear that you won't stick around for long.

Question 175: **What new challenges would you enjoy?**

Answer: I've worked in the hospitality industry for over eight years and have progressively worked in larger, more prestigious hotels. I've learned the food-and-beverage side of the business and the hotel-management side, and now I believe I'm ready to be a convention- or conference-sales manager.

Describe the natural next step in your skill development based on what you've learned and enjoyed in your last job. What do you feel ready to tackle next? Be as specific as you can, considering what you know about the current or future direction of the position and department.

Question 176: **If you could start all over again, what direction would your career take?**

Answer: I've always enjoyed consumer sales as I've moved up in my career. Looking back, I wish I'd gotten a bit more experience in market research earlier in my career, because it's important to understand the types of quantitative models and technical-research techniques that are now important for a regional sales manager to know.

The interviewer will want to see if your career path (including this job interview) is less than ideal for you. Be careful to show that your heart lies in this field, but offer some insights so that someone else following in your footsteps might quicken the learning curve, time frame, and so on.

Question 177:   **What achievements have eluded you?**

Answer: I've achieved considerable success at the finance department of my company, a large corporation. I've worked in two different plants as the director of finance. I've worked in capital budgets at the corporate office and in the business-planning area. Unfortunately, I've never had the opportunity to work in the treasury department. Based on my graduate finance education and my several years' finance experience, I'm now convinced that I'm ready to handle this responsibility and that it'll be the next step in my learning curve toward a top finance-executive position.

Describe a responsibility you'd like but haven't yet earned. What do you feel ready to tackle next? Explain why you haven't yet had the opportunity to assume such a responsibility, but take care not to sound passive. Describe some continuing efforts to reach your goals. Ask yourself, Would your current employer agree that you're ready?

Question 178:   **How long do you think you'd continue to grow in this job?**

Answer: My own personal measure of growth in a job is acquiring new skills, new knowledge, and new insights into the industry. As long as I can measure this type of growth, I consider myself successful. I'm a believer in stretching a job by reaching out to learn more about other areas that are peripheral to the job I'm in.

This is a variation on the question "Where do you want to be in five years?" Be as specific as you can, considering what you know about the position. Don't mention a job title you'd want next, or the interviewer will wonder if you're already preoccupied with moving on.

Question 179: **What career path interests you within the company?**

Answer: I'd like to work toward becoming a senior project manager within your commercial real-estate firm. My background includes several areas within commercial real estate, including working in architectural design, working with governmental departments and agencies, working with banks in the finance area, and, finally, working in sales and leasing. I'd like to pull all this background together in the next few years and eventually have project-management responsibility.

Demonstrate your knowledge of the typical career path, if you're familiar with it. If not, turn this answer into a question: "What's the typical career path for someone with my skills?" Focus principally on businesses or divisions of the company that interest you, as well as skills and challenges you hope to master in the next few years.

Question 180: **Compare this job to others you're pursuing.**

Answer: I've narrowed my job search to only those large securities firms within the finance industry. The basic skills necessary with all of these firms are similar: strong quantitative and analytical abilities, the ability to make decisions quickly, and good interpersonal skills to react to a customer's needs.

Some consistency or thread of commonality among your other prospects is important here. Your choices must reflect your career aspirations. What common skills are clearly needed in all the jobs you're pursuing?

Question 181: **Have you progressed in your career as you expected?**

Answer: My six years with a major gas company have included solid experience in price analysis, capital budgets, and financial planning. I now believe I'm ready to take on departmental responsibility for the entire finance function within a finance company.

Review the positive learning experiences from your past jobs and the next steps you're ready to take as a result, but also be realistic in admitting the areas where you need more experience. Honesty—without demonstrating either pessimism or unrealistic expectations—is important here.

Question 182: **Tell me about your salary expectations.**

Answer: I've become a little frustrated in the past year because the downturn in our industry has caused limited promotional opportunities. Based upon salary information published by our national association, the market price for someone with my experience and educational background is in the broad range of thirty to forty thousand dollars per year. Although I'm not certain how your salaries compare to the national norms, my feeling is that my value would certainly be in the upper half of this national range. I hope you'll share with me some of your salary ranges relative to the national norms.

A well-prepared candidate can effectively turn this question around. Ask first for the company's salary range, then answer in general terms based on your qualifications in relation to the job requirements.

Question 183: **What do you reasonably expect to earn within five years?**

Answer: My expectation for the next five years is that my contributions will be recognized and appropriately rewarded. I realize that salary levels are based on a number of factors, including the company's profitability and the general business cycle that affects our industry, but I expect to take on greater responsibility each year and to be appropriately compensated for my efforts and contributions.

Again, turn this question around and ask what's typical for the career path. Then consider, based on your skills and performance, the areas you'll excel in. Leave it to the interviewer to determine the appropriate time frames for promotions. Don't speculate, or you'll risk sounding arrogant, unrealistic, or the opposite—too reserved or too tentative.

Question 184:   **Have you ever taken a position that didn't fit into your long-term plan?**

Answer: Ten years ago, when Wall Street was booming, I was lured away with a high-paying offer in a firm that was trading commodities on the Asian market. Even though I had success in the job, I quickly realized that the work wasn't fulfilling or challenging enough to keep me happy. So, after two years, I jumped back into the corporate world as a controller for one of the metal plants of my corporation. I've since moved up in the finance area, and my long-term plans include staying in this industry and assuming greater responsibility in the area of financial planning and control.

The interviewer is trying to determine here how wisely the candidate can pick jobs to match his or her interests and aspirations. If you've been sidetracked by some job, you'll probably have to convince the recruiter that you're on the right track pursuing this position.

12. Personal Interests and Hobbies

Question 185: **Other than work, tell me about an activity you've remained interested in over several years.**

Answer: I've been involved in Cancer Society fundraising ever since my grandmother died from the disease. In the back of my mind I guess I'm hoping that the research can lead to findings in time to save the life of someone else in my family.

The interviewer is looking here for a history of commitment over time, and consistency of interests. Do you sustain your hobbies over a period of time, or do you have a different hobby every year? Are your interests compatible with the job you're applying for? Would they be of value in any way to the company?

Question 186: **What do you do in your spare time?**

Answer: I really enjoy getting outside—I often go camping and hiking. I've learned a lot about different fabrics that are good for various weather conditions. That's why I'm so interested in your textile operations.

The interviewer wants evidence that you're well rounded, not just one-dimensional. He or she is also looking for shared interests or common ground. You should always, in some way, relate your answer to the job description.

Question 187: **Do you have a balanced lifestyle?**

Answer: I make an effort to get out of the office at a reasonable hour twice a week. I go home and walk my dog. That's one of the most relaxing things I do, but it often helps me think of solutions for problems at work, even though I'm not consciously trying to solve those problems.

Do you have an outlet, a way to get a break from work, so that you show up each day refreshed and ready to perform at your highest level? Describe something specific that allows you to relax. Are your personal and career interests compatible in terms of their logic or thought processes?

Question 188: **What outside activities complement your work interests?**

Answer: I've always enjoyed tennis. In many ways it's a game of strategy and pacing. When something isn't working in the first set, you have to change your strategy for the second set. You also have to pace your energy in case you go to a third set, and constantly watch and read your opponent's reactions. I'm a gutsy tennis player—I go for the big points sometimes—but I'm careful with timing. That's the way I am at work, too.

The interviewer is interested to see if the candidate's personality is reflected in both work and outside activities. Your answer to this question will shed light on your personality and thus possibly on your compatibility with the job.

Question 189: **Tell me about a time you were in a recreational setting and got an idea that helped in your work.**

Answer: I was on vacation in Mexico and saw a woman with a homemade seesaw she was using to lift her laundry basket when she needed something out of it. It gave me an idea for a new type of scaffolding, which I designed when I got back to work. Now our brick masons have a rotating bench that keeps their materials at waist level, which reduces back fatigue.

The interviewer will want to know if you have the ability to synthesize information and apply what you see to your profession. Show that your work is something you're naturally inquisitive about, rather than something you have to do. Are you able to "think out-side of the box" to come up with fresh ideas? Be sure to give specific examples.

Question 190:   **How is your personality reflected in the kinds of activities you enjoy?**

Answer: I love to cook and entertain. That's the salesman coming out in me. I love sharing experiences with people, and I'm very outgoing. I don't particularly enjoy being alone. I always feel as if I should be doing something.

Describe how your natural skills and values are reflected in various things you do, from work to leisure. What are your comfortable patterns of operating? For example, a detailed, precise hobby reflects something different from a risk-oriented, aggressive sport.

Question 191:   **What kinds of leisure activities help you perform your work better?**

Answer: I enjoy sitting outside during lunch and talking with students. It gives me a chance to get fresh air, but it also helps the students get comfortable with me, so they're more likely to seek my help when they need it.

The recruiter will want to know that you have an outlet to relax. Just about any hobby or leisure activity will help you perform more efficiently at work, but if you can tie the activity directly to job performance, so much the better.

Question 192:   **What do you do to relax?**

Answer: I have a great family. Weekends are like a vacation for me. When I'm at work, I focus on work, but when I'm home on weekends, work really is far from my mind. One of the smartest things I did was to move twenty miles outside of town; even the drive home is relaxing.

An admission that work is far from your mind when you're relaxing is not necessarily a bad thing. This candidate attractively reveals additional information about his or her character and, at the same time, lets the interviewer know that there is plenty of psychic energy stored for the work day.

Question 193: **If you found yourself getting burned out, what would you do to revitalize your energy?**

Answer: I don't allow myself to get involved in a routine to the point that I get burned out. I've always been the type of person who asks for new assignments so that I stay motivated and interested.

Are you disciplined enough to avoid burnout? When you're not being productive, do you recognize it? What do you do to cope with stress?

Question 194: **Our company believes that employees should give time back to the community. How do you feel about it?**

Answer: I believe that, too. In my last job as manager I told each of my employees that they could spend one Friday afternoon a month at a charity of their choice on company time as long as they weren't all gone on the same Fridays. Ironically, productivity didn't decrease at all; they got more done in the morning—and I guess Friday afternoons weren't that productive to begin with. I've spent my afternoons with an adult reading program.

Describe a time you gave something to a community or organization as a volunteer. Do you go above and beyond what's expected of you? Do you use your skills productively? Are you unselfish—a team player? Demonstrate how your personal interests make you productive even when you aren't being paid. What incentives other than a paycheck inspire you?

Question 195: **What community projects that can use your professional skills are particularly interesting to you?**

Answer: As a marketing person, I've offered free advice to our local high school for its fund-raisers, as well as to a local real-estate office whose success could help my rural community's real-estate values.

This interviewer wants to know if the candidate will be a good corporate citizen. The question also gives the interviewer a sense of the job seeker's values. Try to focus your answer on productive applications of your work-related skills. Don't get sidetracked describing a cause that doesn't demonstrate job-related skills. Avoid discussing any charity or organization that may be considered controversial.

Question 196: **If you had unlimited leisure time, how would you spend that time?**

Answer: I don't think I could ever be happy with lots of spare time. I'd probably travel, learn another language, and spend more time with my two charities. I'd also take more courses in accounting.

In answering this question, demonstrate that you'd use your time to increase your skills, or to give something back to the community or a good cause. When possible, choose an activity that's career- or job-oriented; for example, if you're in marketing, say you'd get involved with Junior Achievement and teach young people about careers in business. Your answer should reflect your energy and capacity for work, as well as your natural curiosity. Don't say something like "I don't know; I'd just like to relax."

Question 197: **Describe how a sport or hobby taught you a lesson in teamwork or discipline.**

Answer: My football coach from high school taught me always to watch out for the other guy. If you do, he'll cover you when you need him to. I've applied that principle in all my work groups, especially on the trading floor.

Tell about a time you had to use teamwork to get a desired result. Tell a specific story, then explain how the same skill or lesson has been used in your work.

Question 198: **When you aren't at work, do you prefer to stick to a schedule, or do you prefer to be spontaneous? Why?**

Answer: My workday is very structured because I'm generally in four or five meetings a day. On the weekends, I like to have a plan, but not necessarily a set schedule. That in itself is a relaxing change of pace for me, but I feel I'd be wasting time with no plan at all.

Be careful that, whichever answer you choose, it's consistent with the job you're interviewing for. For example, since accounting is a profession that requires discipline and precision, your answer should reflect your natural inclination toward agendas, schedules, and precision. However, for a sales job, you'd probably want to show that you're prepared to wing it. This question is essentially about your personality but is also about your compatibility with the job.

Question 199: **Tell me about an interest that you outgrew.**

Answer: Early on, I wanted to be a research physician. Then I spent time in a chemistry lab and realized I wasn't looking forward to the next two years of lab work. That's why I've chosen marketing for medical equipment instead. It combines my respect for the medical profession with a job that's more suited to my personality.

Describe a former interest or hobby that you no longer pursue, making sure that the interest isn't related in some way to the job you're interviewing for. Talk about why you outgrew the interest and how it's not compatible with your current interests. Be sure to discuss how your current interests are related to your career.

Question 200: **Describe a movie you've seen that really inspired you.**

Answer: I loved one part of an otherwise depressing movie, *One Flew over the Cuckoo's Nest*. In one scene the nurse refuses to turn on the TV for the World Series, so Jack Nicholson looks at the blank screen and starts narrating as though the game were actually on. The other patients gather around him and follow the game. I thought that scene was an example of the power of visualization in making things happen.

Demonstrate that you can assimilate knowledge from a wide variety of sources, including books and movies. Tell the interviewer about a specific book or movie that taught you something. Discuss how and where you've applied that knowledge.

Chapter 5

50 ZINGERS!

One of the biggest fears that job candidates harbor about interviews is the unanticipated question for which they have no answer. To make matters worse, some recruiters may ask a question knowing full well that you can't possibly answer it. These types of questions are known as stress questions and are designed for their shock effect. Sometimes recruiters ask stress questions not because they enjoy seeing you squirm in your seat, but because they want to judge how well you might react to pressure or tension on the job.

If you encounter a stress question, your best bet is to stay calm, diplomatic, and positive in your response. Don't get defensive or allow your confidence to be shaken, and try to answer the question to the best of your ability. If you simply can't answer the question, think about it for a few seconds. Then, with a confident smile and without apology, simply say, "I can't answer that question."

Following are fifty of the most challenging questions you'll ever face. If you're able to answer these questions, you'll be prepared to handle just about anything the recruiter comes up with.

Question 201: **Tell me about a project in which you were disappointed with your personal performance.**

Answer: In my last job for a manufacturing company, I had to analyze all of the supplier bids and present recommendations to the vice president of logistics. Because the supplier bids weren't in

123

a uniform format, my analysis often consisted of comparing dissimilar items. This caused some confusion in my final report, and by the time I'd reworked it and presented it to the vice president, we'd lost the critical time we needed to improve our approval process for these bids. In hindsight I should have taken a simpler approach to the problem and not tried to make it so complex or all inclusive. Ever since, I've paid more attention to making recommendations in a timely manner.

Describe roadblocks and what you've done to try to get around them. How have your skills come into play? In hindsight, what could you have done differently? What lessons have you learned?

Question 202: **What would you do if I told you that I thought you were giving a very poor interview today?**

Answer: Well, the first thing I'd do is ask you if there was any specific part of the interview that you thought I might have mishandled. After that I'd think back and try to remember if there had been any faulty communication on my part. Then I'd try to review possible problems I had understanding your questions, and I'd ask for clarification if I needed it. Finally, if we had time, I'd try to respond more fully and appropriately to the problem areas you identified for me.

Interviewers like to ask stress questions like these to see how well you hold up under pressure. Your best bet is to stay calm and relaxed; don't allow your confidence to be shaken.

Question 203: **Tell me about your most difficult work or personal experience.**

Answer: One time my coworker went through rehab for six months after a wreck, and I picked up a lot of additional work to help him out. I know he would've done the same for me, and it's important for me to have that kind of trust among the members of my work group.

The interviewer will want to know how you hold up under pressure. Describe a situation, either personal or professional, that involved a great deal of conflict and challenge and placed you under an unusual amount of stress. What, specifically, were the problems, and what did you do to resolve them?

Question 204: **If this were your first annual review with our company, what would I be telling you right now?**

Answer: You'd be thanking me for a job well done and would be explaining how you look forward to continuing to see good work from me. Furthermore, I would anticipate your explaining how you really appreciated my putting in extra time on some key projects and how my creative thinking helped come up with some innovative solutions to existing problems.

For this question you obviously want to present a positive impression. "I wish you would show up on time more," is definitely not a good answer. Remember to focus on one or two of your key strengths based on the personal themes you've developed.

Question 205: **Give an example of a time when you were asked to accomplish a task but weren't given enough information. How did you resolve this problem.**

Answer: At my last internship, my supervisor, an account executive, asked me to assemble five hundred press kits for a mailing. I wasn't sure in what order the pages and press releases should go, but my supervisor had already left for a client meeting. Afraid of putting the information together in the wrong order, I managed to track down her cell-phone number and called her in her car. She explained the order of the materials over the phone, and in the end I managed to prevent a mistake that would have cost hours of work and a delay in the mailing—not to mention a few headaches.

Although this example may seem trivial, the candidate demonstrates maturity and an ability to approach work conceptually. The interviewer will want to know that you understand that just getting the job done isn't enough. Your response should show resourcefulness and initiative.

Question 206: **Describe a time when you failed to resolve a conflict.**

Answer: I wasn't able to keep a good employee once who'd been in our manufacturing facility for ten years. His job description was rewritten to require certain computer skills. I offered to send him to night classes, but he refused the help. I had no option but to replace him. In retrospect, if I'd encouraged him and other employees to acquire new training periodically, he might not have been overwhelmed by the time his position was reworked. Now I'm vigilant about encouraging my group to attend seminars and courses to enhance their job skills and to avoid becoming outdated.

The ideal solution here is to discuss a conflict that wasn't yours to solve in the first place. If you must discuss a personal conflict, focus on the positive steps you'd take if you could go back and do it over again. What have you learned as a result of this experience?

Question 207: **How have you handled criticism of your work?**

Answer: The first time I had a complaint from a client, I found it difficult to keep the complaint separate from my professional service of the account. The client was upset about the downtime on ATM machines. I learned that showing empathy usually calms an unpleasant situation; I also learned that no client is going to be happy with everything, even if that client's overall experience is positive.

The interviewer is looking for an indication of the candidate's accountability and professional character. Describe a specific project or work habit that caused you a problem until you faced up to it and overcame it. Alternatively, you might describe a time you responded objectively and professionally to particularly harsh or unreasonable criticism of your work.

Question 208: **What aspects of your work are most often criticized?**

Answer: I remember in my first job as marketing assistant I spent endless hours analyzing a particular problem. I came up with a revised marketing plan that was extremely well received. Unfortunately, when it came time to present the plan to top management, I hadn't prepared the fine points of the presentation—overheads and slides—and the proposal was turned down. I'd failed to make clear the savings that would result from the plan. I spent the next two weeks working on my presentation, and on my second try management approved it, and my recommendations were carried out to everyone's satisfaction.

This question is similar to the question on weaknesses. Try to give an example from an early job. Discuss what you did to overcome the situation and to improve your work. You could also discuss how the failure has inspired you to pay more careful attention to detail in all your work.

Question 209: **Tell me about the last time you put your foot in your mouth.**

Answer: I told my friend Lisa that I'd no longer be attending yearbook-club meetings because I thought the editor was a complete idiot. I later found out that the editor was her cousin. As soon as I found out, I apologized and asked her why she didn't say anything when I made that foolish comment. Luckily, she and I are still friends today.

Everyone makes mistakes, and it's important for you to be cognizant of yours. The interviewer will want to find out if you have a sense of right and wrong, and what steps you're willing to take to provide restitution for your mistakes. Leaving someone with a bad impression of you, your company, or your client can be very detrimental to your firm.

Question 210: **What might your current boss want to change about your work habits?**

Answer: I'm a morning person and she's a night owl. I like to come into the office at least an hour early, usually by seven, to get a jump start on my work. My boss likes to come in after nine and work late into the evening. So I think if she could change one thing about me, she'd probably make me into a night owl, too, so that I'd be available during many of the same hours she likes to work.

The interviewer will want to know how you'll fit in with your future boss and coworkers, and will also want to feel confident that he or she has uncovered any surprises about your corporate style. One good way to answer this question is to point out minor differences of preference. Alternatively, you might describe a weakness that you and your boss have worked on and improved.

Question 211: **Tell me about two or three aspects of your last job you'd never want to repeat.**

Answer: I'm glad that I have experience in credit collections because it's enabled me to make better risk assessments. I really didn't enjoy the work, though, and it isn't something I want to do again.

In a constructive way, describe two or three things you've done that you didn't especially enjoy or that didn't play upon your strengths. Then describe your strengths and their relevance to the job you're applying for.

Question 212: **Tell me about a situation that frustrated you at work.**

Answer: I was frustrated once when one of my clients, who'd insisted on a high-growth stock, called in a panic because the stock price had dropped more than twenty points in one day. I had a hard time convincing him to ride it out rather than cut his losses. This happened despite my attempts from the beginning to explain the short-term volatility of that stock.

This is another question designed to probe the candidate's professional personality. The interviewer will want reassurance that you are able to hold up under pressure. Describe how you've remained diplomatic, objective, or professional in a difficult situation.

Question 213: **Tell me about one of your projects that failed.**

Answer: I've always had the tendency to be a workaholic, and have the attitude that I can tackle anything and achieve good results. During the hurricane of 1992, my insurance company was inundated with claims. I immediately thought I could handle all the claims in my area and jumped in with both feet to work eighteen-hour days. I quickly realized, though, that there was no way I could complete all of the claims on time, and I had to start to delegate some of the responsibility to my investigators. This experience showed me that no matter how efficient and competent you are, there are times when you must either delegate responsibility or ask for help.

Demonstrate the ability here to be humble and to learn from your mistakes. In hindsight, what could you have done differently? How has your leadership style changed because of the experience?

Question 214: **Tell me about a time when your employer wasn't happy with your job performance.**

Answer: That would be during my first week on the job as a para-legal. I gave her two letters that had typos in them. Frankly, I'd simply been a little sloppy—but that's the only example that comes to mind. Ms. Heilman did tell me regularly that she was very happy with my work.

Again, be sure to discuss a relatively minor incident here. Also, show a willingness to accept responsibility for the problem—don't blame others or make excuses. Simply describe what happened and how you successfully resolved the situation.

Question 215: **Have you ever been passed up for a promotion that you felt you deserved?**

Answer: A couple of times in my early career I thought that I was unfairly passed up for a promotion. However, in retrospect I now realize that in all likelihood I wasn't ready to perform in those jobs—and, in fact, the additional training experience I gained remaining where I was proved invaluable in the last few years, as I've made significant progress moving up the corporate ladder. I've also learned to appreciate that being ready for a promotion doesn't necessarily mean it'll happen. There are many external factors that influence the nature and timing of promotions, aside from a person's performance and capabilities.

The interviewer wants to gauge the candidate's self-confidence, as well as his or her objectivity about personal or professional limitations. Give evidence here that you have enough patience to learn what's important before you get bored or frustrated. After you've mastered your own job, would you stay motivated long enough to be productive?

Question 216: **Have you ever been fired?**

Answer: During one of my summer internships while in college, I worked for a software consulting company. Midway through the summer a new president was appointed because of some financial difficulties, and he requested the resignation of my entire group. I was swept out with everyone else, even though my work performance had never been criticized.

If you've never been fired, of course, this is a simple question to answer. But if you have been fired, you'll need to be prepared to discuss the situation in detail and possibly answer a series of very specific follow-up questions. If the termination was a result of a situation beyond your control, such as corporate downsizing, most interviewers will be very understanding. But if you were fired due to poor performance or some other problem, you'll need to admit your fault and convince the interviewer that you've corrected the problem.

Although this may be a difficult question to answer, you should be completely honest. If you aren't, and the recruiter finds out as much from your references, you may be subject to immediate dismissal, or your job offer may be revoked.

Question 217: **Why have you changed jobs so frequently?**

Answer: My frequent job changes over the last five years have been due to the rapid changes in my profession. My jobs have been based on government contracts, and over the last several years congressional appropriations have been up and down, causing some companies' contracts to be canceled, while other companies land huge, unexpected contracts. This volatility creates some good opportunities, but it also creates a lot of uncertainty. Because your business is based mostly on consumer products, and not on government products, I welcome the opportunity to work in an environment where the business cycle is more stable and predictable.

Be candid here. Personal growth, a larger budget, or other career-enhancing experiences are all valid reasons for moving on. Convince the interviewer that you're interested in his or her company for the long haul.

Question 218: **Why did you stay in your last job so long?**

Answer: I was in my last job over seven years. During that time, I completed an advanced technical degree and also had two six-month assignments in which I was loaned out to different departments. As a result, I acquired some additional skills that normally aren't associated with that particular job. Therefore, I think I've made good progress and am ready to accept the next challenge.

The interviewer may be curious about your interest in personal improvement, tackling new assignments, and so on. He or she may also be concerned about whether you have a tendency to get too comfortable with the status quo. Demonstrate how you've developed job responsibilities in meaningful new ways.

Question 219: **Tell me about a problem you've had getting along with a work associate.**

Answer: I'm pretty easygoing and tend to get along with most people. But I remember one time when we brought in a new associate who was very bossy—to the point where he offended one of our interns with his attitude. I actually pulled him aside and told him that I found it more productive to ask people for help than to give orders. Unfortunately, my advice didn't seem to help much, but we were more careful when we hired new staff after that.

Avoid discussing a personality clash; focus instead on a difference in work ethic between you and an associate, or something else with which the interviewer is likely to empathize. For example, you might describe someone whose standards of excellence were perhaps less stringent than yours.

Question 220: **Tell me about your least-favorite manager or professor.**

Answer: Well, I've been pretty fortunate as far as managers go, and I didn't have any problems with my professors. In my first job out of college I worked with a manager who was pretty inaccessible. If you walked into his office to ask a question, you got the sense that you were bothering him, so we just learned to get help from each other instead. I wouldn't say he was my least-favorite manager, because he was a good manager in a lot of ways, but I would have preferred that he'd made himself more available to us and given us more direction.

Answering this question will be a little bit like walking across a loaded minefield, so beware! Keep in mind that the interviewer doesn't want to learn about your former supervisors; he or she does want to learn about the way you speak about them. Though the interviewer may bait you to make a negative statement about your former employer, doing so can create a host of problems. Even if your claim is completely true and entirely justified, the recruiter may conclude either that you don't get along well with people or that you shift blame to others. The best way around this dilemma is to choose an example that's not too negative, touch upon it briefly, then focus the rest of your answer on what you learned from the experience.

Question 221: **Who's the toughest employer you've ever had, and why?**

Answer: That would be Ms. Henson at Franklin Associates. She'd push people to their limits when things got busy, and she was a stickler for detail. But she was always fair, and she rewarded good, hard work. I'd call her a tough boss, but a good boss.

Again, you should avoid making negative statements about your previous employers, at all costs. Turn the question around with a positive, upbeat response, as this candidate does.

Question 222: **Have you ever had to work with a manager who was unfair to you, or who was just plain hard to get along with?**

Answer: Actually, I've never run into that. Of course, my current boss has to work under time constraints—just like everyone else—and she sometimes has to phrase things succinctly if our department is going to meet its goals. But I've never considered that unfair or hard to handle. It's just part of the job. My supervisors and I have always gotten along quite well.

Never, under any circumstances, criticize a current or former employer, no matter how many times the interviewer gives you the opportunity to do so. What the interviewer is trying to find out here is not whether the candidate has worked for difficult people, but if he or she is willing to bad-mouth them.

Question 223: **Time management has become a necessary factor in productivity. Give an example of a time-management skill you've learned and applied at work.**

Answer: I regularly use scheduling software, which helps me effectively plan for the day, week, month, or year. It also has a to-do-list feature and an alarm option, which is helpful for meeting timely deadlines. In general, though, I'm very goal oriented and self-disciplined. I like to focus clearly on one project at a time for a set amount of hours. In the past I've found that this has helped me save time, which in turn has given me the opportunity to implement new procedures that have ultimately saved the department time and money.

When answering this question, describe a time-management technique you've applied at work that's allowed you to save time and resources. In such areas as public relations time is precious, and the interviewer will want to see that you have an idea of how valuable your time is. Try to give an example that demonstrates how you've managed to increase productivity because of effective time management.

Question 224: **How do you handle tension with your boss?**

Answer: The only tension I've ever felt was once when we both got too busy to keep each other informed. My boss overcommitted me with a short deadline, not knowing that I was bogged down with another client problem. I believe firmly in the importance of staff meetings so that coworkers can respect the demands on each other's time.

The safest ground here is to describe an example of a miscommunication in your early relationship with a boss and how you resolved it. The interviewer will want to know how you avoided a recurrence of the problem.

Question 225: **What would you say are the broad responsibilities of an editorial assistant?**

Answer: Though I'm sure it varies from company to company, I think it would be safe to say that being an editorial assistant involves a lot of typing, filing, and general administrative work. I would probably be expected to read and evaluate book proposals, write manuscript-rejection letters, have some limited correspondence with authors, and generally assist the editor in whatever needed to be done.

You will probably be asked this question in some form or another. This question is similar to "How did the realities differ from your expectations in your last job?" but a little more subtle. Although both questions are basically trying to determine the same thing, this version is a little trickier. Many entry-level applicants have a "glamorized" view of their industry and are unhappily surprised to find themselves performing mundane, clerical tasks. The employer wants to make sure that you have a realistic view of the job and will be likely to be happy in that position for several years.

Question 226: **What is your current salary?**

Answer: I currently earn an annual salary of thirty-five thousand dollars with full benefits.

By all means, if you're asked about your salary history, don't embellish. More and more companies are starting to verify applicants' pay history, some even demanding to see W-2 forms from job seekers. If you get the job, a falsehood discovered even years later may be grounds for immediate dismissal. Don't leave yourself open to this kind of trouble.

Question 227: **Would you be willing to relocate to another city?**

Answer: I'd prefer to be based here, but it's certainly a possibility I'd be willing to consider.

You may, even in some first interviews, be asked questions that seem to elicit a tremendous commitment on your behalf, such as this one. Although such questions may be unfair during an initial job interview, you may well conclude that you have nothing to gain and everything to lose with a negative response. If you're asked such a question unexpectedly during an initial job interview, simply say something like "That's certainly a possibility" or "I'm willing to consider that."

Later, if you receive an offer, you can find out the specific work conditions and then decide if you wish to accept the position. Remember, at the job-offer stage you have the most negotiating power, and the employer may be willing to accommodate your needs. If that isn't the case, you might wish to explain that upon reflection, you've decided you can't (for instance) relocate but you'd like to be considered for other positions that might open up in the future.

Question 228:   **Does the frequent travel required for this work fit into your lifestyle?**

Answer: The frequent travel in this consulting position is no problem for me or my family. My wife is an airline flight attendant, so neither of us follows the typical nine-to-five routine.

If you're comfortable divulging information about your family situation, now is the time to do so. The interviewer is concerned here that the candidate may not be able to travel as much as the job requires. Emphasize your flexibility, or explain why travel wouldn't be a problem, in order to alleviate these concerns.

Question 229:   **Would you be able to work extended hours as necessary to perform the job?**

Answer: I'm accustomed to working long hours during the week. I usually work until at least six-thirty, because I get a lot done after the business office closes at five. I can make arrangements to be available on weekends, if necessary, though I do prefer to have at least twenty-four hours' notice.

Your response should match closely the position you're applying for and should reflect a realistic understanding of the work and time required. Ask about seasonality of work, if you're unsure, and show a willingness to work occasional extended hours.

Question 230: **Sell me this stapler.**

Answer: This is a professional-quality stapler, designed to be functional as well as attractive. It will help you reduce clutter on your desk by enabling you to fasten pages together. And since papers relating to the same subject will now be attached, you'll be more efficient and will save time searching for papers. Finally, its sleek shape and black color are coordinated to match the rest of your office furniture.

With this kind of question the interviewer will want to determine how quickly you think on your feet, as well as your ability to communicate effectively and succinctly. Be prepared to give a thirty-second speech on the benefits and advantages of virtually any common office object, from a paper clip to a telephone, particularly if you're interviewing for a sales position.

Question 231: **How do you feel when things go wrong with a project? How do you handle it?**

Answer: Well, of course I would prefer that my projects run smoothly at all times. However, the very nature of the biotechnology industry means that many changes can and probably will happen to any plan at any time. I try to realize this from the outset and cross each bridge when I come to it. Often I try to have alternate plans ready to go in case of such an event. But sometimes you can't prepare for a problem until it's right there in front of you. Basically I just take it in stride.

This question is tricky. Yet the candidate understands this and has convinced the recruiter that he or she can deal with project setbacks without losing professional composure. The recruiter probably will not ask directly, "Can you work under pressure?" although this is what he or she is after. Responding "I crack under the pressure" to this question is not the way to go.

Question 232: **Prove to me that your interest is sincere.**

Answer: I know that a lot of people want to get into television because of the money or because they just want to be on camera. But to me, communicating well is an art, and the television industry is the ultimate test of how well one communicates. Working in television isn't like working for a newspaper, where if a reader misses a fact, he or she can just go back and reread it. A television news story can go by in a flash, and the challenge is to make sure the audience understands it, learns from it, and, in a broader sense, can use the information to better their lives or their situations. It's the way television can evoke action that's always made me want to be a part of the industry.

I'm particularly interested in this station because I like your focus on the community. Though the on-air products have a great nineties look, it's to your credit that the station seems to remain focused on the tradition of local news and what matters to its audience. The special reports that emphasize town politics, that go on location each week to a different town for a live shot, that explain the big issues facing a community, make the viewer feel that the station is a part of the community. In my opinion this is a great way to maintain a loyal audience.

Being unprepared to answer this question can eliminate you from further consideration. On the other hand, if you're able to demonstrate a strong interest in the company and in the position, you'll have an advantage over the competition.

Question 233: **Tell me about yourself.**

Answer: I'm a production assistant with a B.A. in communications and three years of solid broadcasting and public-relations experience. I have extensive experience developing and researching topics, preinterviewing guests, and producing on-location videotapings. I have a tremendous amount of energy and love to be challenged. I'm constantly trying to take on additional responsibilities and learn new things. I've been watching your station for some time now, and I've been impressed with your innovative approach and your fast growth. I'd like to be a part of that winning team.

This is a perfect opportunity to sell your qualifications to the interviewer. Using the sixty-second pitch you developed in chapter 1 as a guideline, briefly describe your experience, skills, accomplishments, goals, and personal qualities. Explain your interest in the company you're interviewing with and how you plan on making a contribution there. If you're a recent college graduate, be sure to discuss your educational qualifications as well, emphasizing the specific classes you took that are relevant to the position.

Question 234: **What is your biggest weakness?**

Answer: I admit to being a bit of a perfectionist. I take a great deal of pride in my work and am committed to producing the highest-quality work I can. Sometimes if I'm not careful, though, I can go a bit overboard. I've learned that it's not always possible or even practical to try to perfect your work—sometimes you have to decide what's important and ignore the rest in order to be productive. It's a question of trade-offs. I also pay a lot of attention to pacing my work, so that I don't get too caught up in perfecting every last detail.

This is a great example of what's known as a negative question. Negative questions are a favorite among interviewers, because they're effective for uncovering problems or weaknesses. The key to answering negative questions is to give them a positive spin. For this particular question your best bet is to admit to a weakness that isn't catastrophic, inconsistent, or currently disruptive to your chosen professional field, and to emphasize how you've overcome or minimized the problem. Whatever you do, don't answer this question with a cop-out like "I can't think of any," or even worse, "I don't really have any major weaknesses." This kind of response is likely to eliminate you from contention.

Question 235: **You have seven minutes to convince me why you're the best candidate for this position. Go.**

Instead of following a traditional question-and-answer format for a job interview, some recruiters have been known to ask no more than this one question. Only the most prepared candidates will survive this type of interview. If you run into this question, your best bet is to discuss the various sales themes you developed in Chapter 1, emphasizing one or two of your strongest qualifications for the position.

Question 236: **How would you respond to a defaulted form Z–65 counterderivative renewal request if your manager ordered you to do so, and if the policy under which the executive board resolves such issues were currently under review?**

Sometimes recruiters ask seemingly impossible questions just to see how you'll respond. It's not so much that they want to see you squirm in your seat as that they want to judge how you might respond to pressure or tension on the job. No matter how you may feel at the time, being subjected to a ridiculous question like this one is probably a very good sign. If you're asked a tough question that you simply can't answer, think about it for a few seconds. Then, with a confident smile and without apology, simply say something like "I don't know, but if you hire me, I'll sure find out for you."

Special Situations

Interviewing can be even more stressful when you find yourself in what we call a special situation. Perhaps you lack paid job experience, have been out of the workplace to raise children, are concerned about possible discrimination because of age or disability, or are trying to enter a field in which you have no practical experience. Not to worry! The key to improving your chances in an interview is to emphasize your strengths. Focus on your marketable skills (whether they were acquired in the workplace or elsewhere), and highlight impressive achievements, relevant education and training, and/or related interests. And, of course, you should take care to downplay or eliminate any information that may be construed as a weakness.

For example, if you are a "displaced homemaker" (a homemaker entering the job market for the first time), you can highlight the special skills you've acquired over the years while downplaying your lack of paid job experience.

Questions for Students and Recent Graduates

Whether you're graduating from high school or college, those of you with little or no work history face the same dilemma: it's tough to get a job without experience, and it seems impossible to gain experience without getting hired. But, as you'll see, there are ways to get around this problem by emphasizing your strengths and educational achievements.

Question 237: **Why weren't your grades better?**

Answer: School was a wonderful experience for me. I really enjoyed learning new ideas, I studied consistently, and I was attentive in class. But I never believed in cramming before the night of an exam just to get a higher grade or staying up all night to finish a term paper. I really believe I learned just as much as many students who went for the grades.

It's likely that if you've made it to the interview stage, you fulfill the basic criteria for the position, including the education requirements. The recruiter is probably trying to judge here how well the candidate handles adversity. It's important not to get defensive or to place blame. Instead, try to put a positive spin on the question—for example, by concentrating on what you learned and the extra effort you put in, rather than on the grades you received.

Question 238: **Why did you decide to major in history?**

Answer: It was a difficult choice because I was also attracted to government, international relations, and economics. But the study of history allowed me to combine all three, especially by focusing on economic history. What's more, I found several of the professors in the department to be exceptionally knowledgeable and stimulating.

Show that you have solid, logical reasons for choosing your major. If you can't defend your choice of major, the interviewer will wonder how much thought you've put into choosing a career. You should also be sure that your reasons for choosing your major are compatible with your career choice. For instance, don't say you were an English major because you love literature and writing if you're applying for a position as a banker.

Question 239: **Was there a course that you found particularly challenging?**

Answer: Initially I was completely overwhelmed by the introductory chemistry course that I took last year. No matter how hard I studied, I seemed to be getting nowhere. I failed the first three quizzes. So I tried a new approach. Instead of just studying by myself, I asked a friend who's a chemistry major to help me with my studies. I also began seeking help from the professor after class. And I found that more time spent in the lab was critical. I ended up with a B-plus in the course and thought I achieved a solid understanding of the material. More than that, I learned that tackling a new field of study sometimes requires a new approach, not just hard work, and that the help of others can be crucial!

The interviewer will want to see how well you respond to difficult situations. Demonstrate that you won't fold in the face of difficulty, and that you're willing to put in the extra effort to meet a challenge.

Question 240: **Why didn't you participate more in extracurricular activities?**

Answer: I wanted to give as much effort as possible to my studies. I came from a high school in a very small town, where I received a lot of A's, but this didn't prepare me very well for college. So I studied very hard. I have, however, found time to explore the city and make new friends, and I do socialize informally on weekends.

The interviewer may be worried that if you don't have many outside interests, you may eventually suffer from burnout. Employers like candidates who are well rounded and have interests outside of work. If you didn't participate in formal extracurricular activities in college, you still may want to talk about some of your interests, such as reading or exercising, that you participated in on a more informal level. For instance, you may have a passion for running even if you weren't on the college track team.

Questions for Career Changers

For those of you who've devoted your careers exclusively to one profession or industry, work experience really isn't an issue. You have lots of experience—but none of it relates to your current job objective. No problem! Instead of emphasizing your job history, you'll just have to emphasize the skills you've acquired that apply to the job you're seeking. For example, let's say your career has been in real estate and, in your spare time, you like to run in marathons. Recently you heard about an opening in the sales-and-marketing department at an athletic-shoe manufacturer. What you need to do is emphasize the skills you have that the employer is looking for. Not only do you have strong sales experience, you're familiar with the needs of the company's market, and that's a powerful combination!

Question 241: **Why do you want to leave your current position?**

Answer: I've learned quite a bit about the plastics industry in my current position and am very glad to have had the opportunities I've had at Fiske, Inc. However, I've found that my interests really lie in research and development, which Fiske has recently decided to phase out over the next two years. And that's why I'm so interested in this organization, because, as I understand, Randy Corporation places a great deal of emphasis on R&D, and is also a highly respected leader in the industry.

The interviewer's foremost concern with career changers will always be why they want to switch careers. Show the interviewer that your decision has been based on careful consideration. Explain why you decided upon this particular position, as well as how the position will allow you to further your natural skills and interests.

Question 242: **Why would you want to leave an established career at an employment agency for an essentially entry-level position in marketing?**

Answer: I've enjoyed my work at the agency and have gained many valuable skills from it. At the same time, however, I feel as if I've stopped growing. I'm no longer challenged by my work. I've thought about this for a long time, and I'm confident that it's time for a change.

As for my interest in marketing, last year my teenage children and some of the other neighborhood kids decided to design and sell T-shirts to benefit a local family who'd lost their home to a fire. I pitched in by designing and distributing posters, placing advertisements in local newspapers, and selling shirts outside grocery stores and shopping malls. At first I really didn't give the project a lot of thought, but when I saw the fruits of my labor, I began to get very excited about it. I learned that you can have a great product and a great cause, but if nobody knows about it, you're dead in the water. I finally felt as if I was making a difference—and I was good at it, too. Since then I've taken two introductory marketing courses and am planning to enroll in a part-time degree program this fall.

Furthermore, I'll be able to use many of the skills and abilities I've gained at the employment agency in the marketing field. After all, working for an employment agency is marketing—marketing the agency to corporate clients and job seekers, and marketing job seekers to corporate clients.

The interviewer is trying to determine two things: the candidate's motivation for choosing a new career, and the likelihood that the candidate will be comfortable in a position where he or she will probably have less power and responsibility than in previous jobs. To dispel the interviewer's fears, discuss your reasons for switching careers, and be sure to show that you have a solid understanding of the position and the industry in general. Many candidates expect to start their new careers in a job comparable to the one they held previously. But the truth is that most career changers must start in lower—if not entry-level—positions in their new company to gain basic experience and knowledge of the field.

Questions for Candidates Re-entering the Job Market

There's no doubt about it, if you've been out of the workforce for a while, you're facing some troubling issues. You may be feeling anxious, wondering if you've still got what it takes to make it out there. The key element for you is to make sure all of your skills are up-to-date. If they aren't, you should consider retraining, which might mean learning a new computer program or taking a class at the local college. If your skills are current, not to worry. What you'll need to emphasize is your previous job experience and skills, ways you've kept up-to-date during your leave (reading trade journals, doing freelance work, attending seminars), and the skills you've learned at home that can be transferred to the workplace.

Question 243: **Your resume doesn't list any job experience in the past few years. Why not?**

Answer: I took five years off to raise my son, Jason, who's now in kindergarten. It was a difficult decision for me, but at the time, I decided I wouldn't be able to commit myself 100 percent to my career with such tremendous responsibilities at home. And I didn't think it would be fair to my employer to give any less than my complete and total commitment. I believe it was the right decision for me at the time, but now I feel refreshed and ready to devote myself full-time to my career.

Whatever the reason for your hiatus, be honest. Discuss the decisions behind your absence, whether they were to stay home and raise a family or to recuperate from a debilitating injury. Tell the interviewer why you're now ready to return to work. Most important, emphasize your eagerness to resume your career.

Question 244: **I see you've been out of work for a while. What difficulties have you had in finding a job that's compatible with your interests?**

Answer: It's true that I've been out of my field for the last four years, but I've had a number of tempting offers to jump back in. However, I thought it was important to stay home with my new baby and also continue a part-time family business, which I ran out of our home while my husband was completing law school. Now that that's behind us, I'm ready to return to my career in the entertainment industry.

The real question behind the interviewer's curiosity here is why someone else hasn't taken this candidate off the market. Why isn't the candidate in greater demand? Is he or she being too unrealistic or perhaps going after random positions? Is there something in the job seeker's past that others have discovered? You'll need to alleviate such concerns by frankly discussing your situation. Be sure to emphasize how you've remained involved in your career during your sabbatical, as well as your eagerness to rejoin the workforce.

Question 245: **Your resume indicates that you've been working for the past two years as a part-time clerk at Reliable Insurance Brokers. How will this experience help you in your banking career?**

Answer: Reliable was in the process of computerizing its files, and I was hired primarily to check the computerized files for accuracy vis-à-vis the manual files. I recorded premium payments, prepared bank deposits, and sorted payables. Not only did this work help me keep my accounting skills current, I also learned valuable computer skills that will certainly help me become even more efficient and productive in my next position in banking.

The interviewer may be concerned here that the candidate is simply applying for any available job, rather than for a specific position in a specific field. Explain how your experience relates to the position you're applying for, and discuss any skills you've gained that are transferable to the position and company.

Illegal Interview Questions

Illegal interview questions probe into your private life or personal background. Federal law forbids employers from discriminating against any person on the basis of sex, age, race, national origin, or religion. For instance, an interviewer may not ask you about your age or your date of birth. However, she or he may ask you if you're over eighteen years of age.

If you're asked an illegal question at a job interview, keep in mind that many employers simply don't know what's legal and illegal. One strategy is to try to discover the concerns behind the question and then address them. For instance, if the employer asks you about your plans to have children, he or she may be concerned that you won't be able to fulfill the travel requirements of the position. Sexist? You bet. But it's to your advantage to try to alleviate those concerns.

Try to get to the heart of the issue behind the question by saying something like "I'm not quite sure I understand what you're getting at. Would you please explain to me how this issue is relevant to the position?" Once the interviewer's real concerns are on the table, you can allay those concerns by saying something like "I'm very interested in developing my career. Travel is definitely not a problem for me—in fact, I enjoy it tremendously. Now, let me direct your attention to my experience and expertise in . . ."

Alternatively, you may choose to answer the question or to gracefully point out that the question is illegal and decline to respond. Avoid reacting in a hostile fashion—remember that you can always decide later to decline a job offer.

Any of the following responses are acceptable ways to handle these tricky situations without blowing your chances for a job offer. Choose the response that's most comfortable for you.

Question 246: **What religion do you practice?**

Answer 1:   I make it a point not to mix my personal beliefs with my work, if that's what you mean. I assure you that I value my career too much for that.

Answer 2:   I'm not quite sure I understand what you're getting at. Would you please explain to me how this issue is relevant to the position?

Answer 3:   That question makes me uncomfortable. I'd really rather not answer it.

Question 247: **How old are you?**

Answer 1: I'm in my fifties and have over thirty years of experience in this industry. My area of expertise is in . . .

Answer 2: I'm too young to retire, but I'm old enough to know better than to answer a question like that.

Answer 3: I'm not quite sure I understand what you're getting at. Would you please explain to me how this issue is relevant to the position?

Answer 4: That question makes me uncomfortable. I'd really rather not answer it.

Question 248: **Are you married?**

Answer 1: No.

Answer 2: Yes, I am. But I keep my family life separate from my work life so that I can put all my effort into my job. I'm flexible when it comes to travel and late hours, as my references can confirm.

Answer 3: I'm not quite sure I understand what you're getting at. Would you please explain to me how this issue is relevant to the position?

Answer 4: That question makes me uncomfortable. I'd really rather not answer it.

Question 249: **Do you have children?**

Answer 1: No.

Answer 2: Yes, I do. But I keep my family life separate from my work life so that I can put all my effort into my job. I'm flexible when it comes to travel and late hours, as my references can confirm.

Answer 3: I'm not quite sure I understand what you're getting at. Would you please explain to me how this issue is relevant to the position?

Answer 4: That question makes me uncomfortable. I'd really rather not answer it.

Question 250: **Do you plan to have children?**

Answer 1: No.

Answer 2: It's certainly a consideration, but if I do, it won't be for some time. I want to do the best job I can for this company and have no plans to leave just as I begin to make meaningful contributions.

Answer 3: I can't answer that right now. But if I ever do decide to have children, I wouldn't let it detract from my work. Becoming a parent is important, but my career is certainly very important to me, too. I plan on putting all of my efforts into this job and this company.

Answer 4: I'm not quite sure I understand what you're getting at. Would you please explain to me how this issue is relevant to the position?

Answer 5: That question makes me uncomfortable. I'd really rather not answer it.

PART 3

After the Interview

Chapter 6

CLINCHING THE DEAL

You've made it through the toughest part—but now what? First, breathe a sigh of relief! Then, as soon as you've left the interview site, write down your thoughts about the interview while they're still fresh in your mind. Ask yourself these key questions:

- What does the position entail?
- What do you like and dislike about the position and the company?
- Did you make any mistakes or have trouble answering any of the questions?
- Did you feel you were well prepared?
- If not, what could you do to improve your performance in the future?

Carefully consider all of these questions; if you find that your performance was lacking, work to improve it.

Be sure to keep a file with the name and title of the person you interviewed with, as well as the names and titles of anyone else you may have met. Ideally, you'll have collected their business cards. Don't forget to write down what the next agreed-upon step will be. Will the recruiter contact you? How soon?

Writing Your Follow-Up E-mail

It's fair to say that follow-up e-mails won't necessarily help you secure the job, but not sending one will most certainly hurt your chances. You should write an e-mail immediately after each interview you have, ideally within twenty-four hours. The e-mail should be brief (no more than two or three paragraphs) and personalized. In your e-mail, you should be sure to:

- Express your appreciation for the opportunity to interview with the recruiter.
- Express your continued enthusiasm about the position and the company.
- Recap your strengths, being careful to relate them to the requirements of the job and the company.
- Request to meet again.

The following is an example of a good follow-up letter. You can send a hardcopy or adapt the text for an e-mail.

Sample Follow-Up Letter

178 N. Green Street
Chicago, IL 60657
(312) 555-5555
(312) 555-5050
csmith96@aol.com

December 1, 20—

Pat Cummings
Personnel Manager
Any Corporation
1140 State Street
Chicago, IL 60601

Dear Ms. Cummings:

It was a pleasure meeting with you yesterday regarding the research-assistant position. I enjoyed learning more about the opportunity and about Any Corporation.

The position is exciting and seems to encompass a diversity of responsibilities. I believe that with my experience and skills, I'm qualified to make a valuable contribution to your organization.

Should you require additional information, please don't hesitate to contact me at either telephone number listed above or at (312) 555-1212. You can also e-mail me at the above address.

I look forward to hearing from you.

Sincerely,

Chris Smith

Chris Smith

Allow the interviewer five to ten business days to contact you after receiving your e-mail If you still haven't heard anything after that time, you should follow up with a phone call. Express your continued interest in the firm and the position, and inquire as to whether or not a decision has been made or when you'll be notified.

In the meantime, it's important to keep your candidacy fresh in the interviewer's mind. Send work that intrigued the interviewer (for example, brochures or writing samples). If the conversation during the interview provided any possibilities for follow-up, such as reading an article or book, send a note to the interviewer, mentioning how much you learned from the piece. Or if you discovered during the interview that you share common interests with the interviewer, such as sailing or rock climbing, consider sending the person a great article you just found on the topic. Not only will this ensure that you don't get lost in the shuffle, it will help you establish a sense of camaraderie with the interviewer. Though this technique won't guarantee you the position, it certainly can't hurt if it gets the interviewer in your corner!

Taking the Next Step

Don't be discouraged if you don't receive an immediate response from an employer—most companies interview many applicants before making a final decision. Take advantage of this time to contact other firms, and to schedule more interviews, so that if a rejection does come, you have other options open. Continuing to job-hunt and to interview will have been a good idea even if you end up receiving the job offer. Ultimately, you may have a number of opportunities to choose from, and you'll be in a better position to negotiate terms.

If you place too much importance on a single interview, not only are you bound to be unduly disappointed if the offer doesn't come through, you'll be wasting valuable time and energy. So keep plugging away!

Handling Rejection

Rejection is inevitable, and it's bound to happen to you just as it happens to all other job hunters. The key is to be prepared for it and not to take it personally.

One way you can turn rejection around is by contacting each person who sends you a rejection letter. Thank your contact for considering you for the position and request that he or she keep you in mind for future openings. If you feel comfortable, you may want to ask the person for suggestions to help you improve your chances of getting a job in that industry or for the names of people who might be looking for someone with your skills. You may want to say something like "What would you do in my situation? Whom would you call?"

Two cautions are in order: First, don't ask employers to tell you why they didn't hire you. Not only will this place a recruiter in a very awkward position, you'll probably get a very negative reaction. Second, keep in mind that if you contact employers solely for impartial feedback, not everyone will be willing to talk to you.

A well-written thank-you e-mail, sent within one or two days of receiving notice of rejection, makes a positive statement. When Danny P. was turned down for a position as a publicity director, he quickly wrote his interviewer a letter that expressed his disappointment at not being offered the job, but also his thanks for the company's consideration of his qualifications. The interviewer was so impressed by Danny's initiative, she provided him several contact names to assist in his continued search.

In your letter, emphasize an ongoing interest in being considered for future openings. Also, be very careful to use an upbeat tone. Although you may be disappointed, you don't want to put the employer on the defensive or imply that you don't respect his or her decision. Above all, don't give up! Stay positive and motivated, and learn from the process. Success could be right around the corner!

Chapter 7

THE ART OF NEGOTIATION

In today's tough economy, one of the most nerve-racking steps on the trail to a new job is near the end of the path: deciding whether or not to accept an offer. On the one hand, if you've been in the job market for some time, your instincts may scream, "I'll take it! I'll take it!" before the last syllables of the offer are out of the recruiter's mouth. On the other, you may also be worrying that the salary won't even cover the cost of all those stamps you've used to send out resumes and cover letters over the past few months.

Faced with these conflicting emotions, many job seekers can make unnecessary, costly mistakes during this final, vitally important stage. Far too many people sell themselves short without even exploring their options. Others have wildly unrealistic expectations of the level of compensation they should expect. Still others get so wrapped up in money questions they forget to consider other issues—a big mistake.

Important Factors to Consider

If you're going to consider a job offer seriously, be confident that this is a job you really want. If you're just graduating, is the job in the field you'd like to pursue? Are you willing to live and work in the area in question? Would you enjoy the work schedule? The way of life?

Whether or not a job will help your career progress is ultimately a much more important question than what your starting salary will be. In some organizations, you may be given a lot of responsibility right away but then find your upward progress blocked. Make sure you know if there are opportunities for advancement. Ask about performance reviews: how often are they conducted?

Other information you should have in order to make a sound decision includes:

- Start date
- Job title and associated responsibilities
- Salary, overtime, and compensation
- Bonus structure
- Tuition reimbursement
- Vacation and parental-leave policy
- Life-, medical-, and dental-insurance coverage
- Pension plan
- Travel requirements

Ideally, these issues will have been covered during the course of the interview process or at the time the job offer is made. But if you're unsure of any of this information, don't assume that the specifics will be to your satisfaction. Contact the personnel representative or recruiter and confirm all important details.

Work Environment

Another important factor to consider is the kind of environment you'll be working in. Is the company's atmosphere comfortable, challenging, and exciting? Consider specifics, including office or workstation setting, privacy, proximity to other staff, amount of space, noise level, and lighting. How much interaction occurs between coworkers? Some organizations strongly encourage teamwork and dialogue among staff, whereas others prefer to emphasize individual accomplishment. Which approach works better for you? Remember: If you don't like the work environment before you accept the job, you probably won't like it as an employee.

Salary and Benefits

Money may seem like the biggest criterion in accepting a job, but it can often cloud the decision-making process. Don't accept a job that you're not enthusiastic about simply because the starting salary is a few thousand dollars higher than what you're currently making. It's probably more important to find a job that lets you do something you enjoy. Ask yourself whether the position presents a career path with upward movement and long-range income potential.

Benefits can make a big difference in your compensation package, so don't overlook them! Perhaps the most important benefit to consider is health insurance. With health-insurance costs skyrocketing, you should be sure to find out if the company covers these costs in full. If the company, like many others, pays only a percentage of these costs, make certain that you can afford to pay the difference out of your own pocket.

And what about life, dental, and disability insurance? Does the company have a bonus structure or profit-sharing plan? These things can contribute significantly to your salary. Is there a pension plan? How many vacation days or sick days will you get? You should consider all of these factors carefully.

If you plan to continue your education, it's important to find out if the organization will pay for your tuition and if the employer will give you time to attend classes. Some organizations offer tuition incentives but require so much overtime that it's very difficult to take advantage of the benefit.

Do Your Homework

Supplement the information that the organization provides by searching journals and newspapers for articles about the company and, if possible, by talking to current employees. Try to get objective comments—not, for instance, information from someone who was recently fired by the company. Alumni of your college or university who hold similar positions or are employed by the same organization may be an excellent source of information.

Negotiating the Offer

The prospect of negotiating salary and benefits strikes fear into the hearts of many job seekers young and old. But handling the inevitable money questions doesn't have to be difficult. And the more you think about them in advance, the easier they'll be for you to answer. Let's go through the process step by step.

First, the basics. Never try to negotiate salary or benefits until after you've gotten an offer. Try it, and you'll look as if you care more about money than about putting your skills to work for the company. Your goals at an interview are simple: (1) prove to the recruiter that you're well-suited to the job as you understand it, and (2) make sure that you feel comfortable with the prospect of performing the job and working in the environment the company offers.

If you've been offered a position, congratulations! The hard part is over. If you feel uncomfortable about negotiating for a salary, relax. The tables are now turned in your favor. Think about it—you've already gotten what you want. Until you say yes to the offer, the burden is on the recruiter. He or she has put a lot of time and effort into finding the right candidate and has decided that you are that person. If you say no, the recruiter will have wasted a lot of energy and may have to go back to square one to find another candidate.

So don't worry about the recruiter's withdrawing his or her handshake and showing you the door if you dare to ask if the company's offer is flexible. The worst case might be that the employer tells you your salary is set by company policy and there's really no room to negotiate. But the recruiter may just as likely tell you he or she can't give you an immediate answer and will have to get back to you.

The most important thing to remember about salary negotiations is that most salaries are negotiable. That doesn't mean that you name a figure and the employer either matches it or doesn't. It means that you're ready to listen to what the recruiter has to offer, and give it consideration. To succeed in negotiation, both parties have to reach an agreement with which both are happy. If you somehow succeed at winning yourself a bigger paycheck but antagonize your future boss in doing so, trouble lies ahead. If, on the other hand, you set realistic expectations and realize that you may not get everything you want, you'll probably do just fine.

Just how do you know how much you should expect? The answer is the same as in every other step of your job search: Do your homework. Contact your professional association or read the trade journals for your industry. Call employment agencies to find out salaries of jobs listed with them; read the newspaper help-wanted ads. Alumni of your college or university in similar positions (or employed by the same organization) may also be an excellent source of information. Doing this research will give you an idea of the general salary level you can realistically expect.

Setting realistic expectations is especially important for the entry-level job seeker or recent graduate. If you don't have a lot of professional experience, you don't leave the recruiter with much hard evidence on which to base a decision. Instead, you're asking him or her to take a leap of faith based on potential that you've demonstrated in classes, internships, volunteer work, or extracurricular activities. Without a track record of professional experience, your arsenal is missing a powerful weapon. This is why entry-level salaries are often determined by the marketplace. That leaves you very little leverage with which to negotiate. Even so, that doesn't mean you can't give it a try.

On the other hand, if you have some experience under your belt and are looking for a midlevel or executive-level position, your negotiating power might be much greater. For a lucky (or unlucky) few at the top of the heap, salary and benefit negotiations can be as complex and painstakingly slow as a bill passing through Congress. If you're like most people, you're not in that group. Whatever your level of experience, your task is to try to figure out just how high the employer is likely to go.

If, after listening politely to the specifics of the offer, you're left hoping for a higher salary, greater health coverage, or something else, it's okay to say so (calmly). Find out if the offer is firm. If it seems there may be some room to negotiate, make sure you have a specific figure in mind, because if the recruiter does have the freedom to barter, he or she will probably ask you point-blank to supply a figure that would satisfy you.

When you're asked that question, rule number one is as follows: Don't tip your hand by giving the interviewer a concrete number for which you're willing to settle. You don't want to take yourself out of the running by naming a figure that's absurdly optimistic, and you certainly don't want to risk naming a figure that's lower than what the employer is ready to offer. Instead of naming your price, say something like, "Based on my experience and skills, and the demands of the position, I'd expect to earn an appropriate figure. Can you give me some idea what kind of range you have in mind?"

If you're pressed about salary requirements during an interview and you feel you must name a figure, give a salary range instead of your most recent salary. And don't forget to add in the value of your insurance, pension, or any other benefits you had.

Naming a salary range gives you a chance to hook on to a figure that's also in the range the company has in mind. In fact, many companies base their offers on sliding salary scales. Therefore, if you name a range of, say, twenty-five to thirty thousand dollars, it just may be that the company was considering a range of twenty-two to twenty-eight thousand dollars. In this case, you'll be more likely to receive an offer in the mid-to-upper end of your range. Of course, your experience and qualifications also play a part here. If you're just starting out and have little experience, the recruiter may be more likely to stick toward the lower end of the scale.

A few words about projecting the right attitude when discussing money—try not to reveal what you're thinking. Even if the salary offer seems barely above poverty level, it wouldn't be wise to inform the recruiter of that fact. Similarly, if the offer is much higher than you expected, doing cartwheels around the room probably wouldn't be appropriate, either.

In all seriousness, though your appearance and demeanor are important throughout your career, they are especially important at the interview and offer stages. If you want to be a professional, start right away by acting like one.

Some final notes. The point of your job search isn't salary negotiation; it's finding a job that you'll be happy with, that you'll grow with, and that will allow you to be yourself. If your starting salary isn't the one you dreamed about, but the job presents the right opportunity, think about the possibility of commanding a higher salary once you've had a chance to make yourself invaluable to the organization.

On the other hand, if the salary or benefits fall far short of your realistic expectations, despite all your efforts to negotiate, nothing says you have to take the job. Don't make the mistake of accepting a position with which you're fundamentally unhappy. Trust your instincts—if you're dissatisfied with the employer before your start date, don't bet that the situation will improve after you start.

THE 250 QUESTIONS

The Basic Interview Questions

1. Passion for the Business

#1: Why do you want to work in this industry?

#2: Why would you be particularly good at this business?

#3: How do you stay current?

#4: Why do you think this industry would sustain your interest over the long haul?

#5: Where do you want to be in five years?

#6: Describe your ideal career.

#7: If you had unlimited time and financial resources, how would you spend them?

2. Motivation and Purpose

#8: Tell me something about yourself that I didn't know from reading your resume.

#9: Tell me what you know about this company.

#10: What have you learned about our company from customers, employees, or others?

#11: Why do you want to work here?

#12: What particular aspect of the company interests you most?

#13: What's your favorite product made by our company?

#14: What do you think of our newest product and ads?

#15: Tell me what you think our distinctive advantage is within the industry.

#16: Where do you think we're the most vulnerable as a business?

#17: What would you do differently if you ran the company?

#18: What other firms are you interviewing with, and for what positions?

#19: Do you believe you're overqualified for this position?

#20: Describe our competition as you see it.

#21: What would you do if one of our competitors offered you a position?

#22: Why are you ready to leave your current job?

#23: What do you want out of your next job?

#24: What's your dream job?

#25: What motivates you to do this kind of work?

#26: What salary would you expect for this job?

#27: What new skills or ideas do you bring to the job that other candidates aren't likely to offer?

#28: What interests you most about this job?

#29: What would you like to accomplish that you weren't able to accomplish in your last position?

#30: We have a number of applicants interviewing for this position. Why should we take a closer look at you?

#31: How have your career motivations changed over the past few years?

#32: Why should I hire you?

3. Skills and Experience

#33: What are your key skills?

#34: What sets you apart from the crowd?

#35: What are your strengths?

#36: How is your experience relevant to this job?

#37: What skills do you think are most critical to this job?

#38: What skills would you like to develop in this job?

#39: If you had to stay in your current job, what would you spend more time on? Why?

#40: How could you enrich your current job?

#41: How do you explain your job successes?

#42: Compared to others with a similar background in your field, how would you rate yourself?

#43: How good are your writing abilities?

#44: What computer systems and software do you know?

4. Diligence and Professionalism

#45: Give an example of how you saw a project through, despite obstacles.

#46: Share an example of your determination.

#47: Share an example of your diligence or perseverance.

#48: Describe a time when you tackled a tough or unpopular assignment.

#49: Would your current boss describe you as the kind of employee who goes the extra mile?

#50: How many days were you absent from work last year? Why?

#51: Tell me about a time you didn't perform to your capabilities.

#52: Employees tend to be either concept oriented or task oriented. How do you describe yourself?

#53: What would your colleagues tell me about your attention to detail?

#54: How do you manage stress in your daily work?

#55: How do you regroup when things haven't gone as planned?

#56: How have you prioritized or juggled your workload in your current job?

#57: Describe a professional skill you've developed in your most recent job.

#58: Why is service such an important issue?

#59: Tell me about a time when you had to deal with an irate customer. How did you handle the situation?

#60: Are there any issues from your personal life that might have an impact on your professional career?

#61: When have your skills in diplomacy been put to the test?

#62: How do you manage your work week and make realistic deadlines?

#63: Tell me about a time you had to extend a deadline.

#64: What personal skill or work habit have you struggled to improve?

#65: What books do you keep on your desk?

5. Creativity and Leadership

#66: What color is your brain?

#67: If you got on an elevator where everyone was facing the back, what would you do?

#68: What's the most creative or innovative project you've worked on?

#69: Describe a time when you've creatively overcome an obstacle.

#70: Consider the following scenario: You're working late one evening and are the last person in the office. You answer an urgent telephone call to your supervisor from a sales rep who's currently meeting with a potential client. The sales rep needs an answer to a question to close the sale. Tomorrow will be too late. You have the expertise to answer the question, but it's beyond your normal level of authority. How would you respond?

#71: Why do you think that some companies with good products fail?

#72: How resourceful are you?

#73: Give me proof of your persuasiveness.

#74: What would your last supervisor say about your initiative?

#75: Describe an improvement you personally initiated.

#76: Describe a time in your work experience when the existing process didn't work and what you did about it.

#77: Describe a time you had to alter your leadership style.

#78: Tell me about a good process that you made even better.

#79: Tell me about a time you persuaded others to adopt your idea.

#80: How would a former colleague or subordinate describe your leadership style?

#81: Do you believe that your job appraisals have adequately portrayed your leadership abilities?

#82: Describe the situations in which you're most comfortable as a leader.

#83: Describe your comfort level working with people of higher rank and people of lower rank.

6. Compatibility with the Job

#84: What were the most rewarding aspects of your most recent job?

#85: What are the limitations of your current job?

#86: What do you want to achieve in your next job?

#87: Describe your ideal job.

#88: What interests you most about this job?

#89: What interests you least about this job?

#90: What aspects of this job do you feel most confident about?

#91: What concerns you most about performing this job?

#92: What skills do you offer that are most relevant to this job?

#93: Considering your own resume, what are your weaknesses in relation to this job?

#94: How did the realities differ from your expectations in your last job?

#95: How would you enrich your current (or most recent) job?

#96: Would you be able to travel as necessary to perform the job?

#97: Why is this a particularly good job for someone with your qualifications?

#98: What's your most productive or ideal work setting?

#99: Do you prefer continuity in structure or frequent change in your daily work?

7. Personality and Cultural Compatibility

#100: What would your friends tell me about you?

#101: Tell me about your relationship with your previous bosses.

#102: Describe your working relationship with your colleagues.

#103: Describe your personality beneath the professional image.

#104: What environments allow you to be especially effective?

#105: Describe an environment that is ineffective for you.

#106: What situations excite and motivate you?

#107: How would your last employer describe your work habits and ethics?

#108: How do you feel your company treats its employees?

#109: Did your customers or clients enjoy working with you?

#110: How will you complement this department?

#111: Whom did you choose as your references, and why?

#112: Can we call all of your references?

#113: Tell me what you learned from a recent book.

#114: Tell me about a work group you really enjoyed.

#115: Describe a time when you had to assist a coworker.

#116: Are you most productive working alone or in a group?

#117: Tell me about a situation in which it was difficult to remain objective.

8. Management Style and Interpersonal Skills

#118: Tell me about an effective manager, supervisor, or other person in a leading role you've known.

#119: What type of management style do you think is effective?

#120: Describe your personal management style.

#121: What type of people do you work with most effectively?

#122: What things impress you in colleagues?

#123: What are some of the things your supervisor did that you disliked?

#124: How do you organize and plan for major projects?

#125: Describe a time when you've worked under intense pressure.

#126: How do you manage your time on a typical day?

#127: Describe a time when you acted on someone's suggestion.

#128: Tell me about a time when you had to defend an idea to your boss.

#129: What aspect of your management style would you like to change?

#130: Have you ever felt defensive around your boss or peers?

#131: Tell me about a learning experience that affected your management style.

#132: Have you patterned your management style after someone in particular?

#133: Describe a leader you admire.

#134: What personal characteristics add to your effectiveness?

9. Problem-Solving Ability

#135: How have your technical skills been an asset?

#136: Describe a situation in which you've applied technical skills to solve a problem.

#137: How do your technical skills, combined with other skills, add to your effectiveness on the job?

#138: Describe how you've used a problem-solving process.

#139: How do you usually go about solving a problem?

#140: How do you measure the success of your work?

#141: How practical or pragmatic are you?

#142: How do you balance your reliance on facts with your reliance on intuition?

#143: What was your greatest problem in your last job?

#144: Tell me about a problem that you failed to anticipate.

#145: Have you ever resolved a long-standing problem?

#146: Describe a time you found it necessary to make an unpopular decision.

#147: Tell me about the most difficult problem you've ever dealt with.

#148: Describe a time when a problem wasn't resolved to your satisfaction.

#149: Tell me about a time when there was no rule or precedent to help you attack a problem.

#150: When do you have difficulty making choices?

#151: Describe an opportunity in which you felt the risks far outweighed the rewards.

10. Accomplishments

#152: Tell me about a major accomplishment.

#153: Talk about a contribution you've made to a team.

#154: Talk about a special contribution you've made to an employer.

#155: Tell me about an organization outside of work that's benefited from your participation.

#156: Give me an example of a time you delivered more than was expected.

#157: What accomplishment is your greatest source of pride?

#158: If I hired you today, what would you accomplish first?

#159: What accomplishment was the most difficult for you to achieve?

#160: Tell me about a time you saved money for an employer or an organization.

#161: What's your greatest achievement to date?

#162: Tell me about a person or group you had to work with to achieve something important.

#163: Tell me about something you accomplished that required discipline.

#164: What situations do your colleagues rely on you to handle?

#165: Tell me about a need you fulfilled within a group or a committee.

#166: Tell me how you've supported and helped attain a corporate goal.

#167: Tell me about a quantifiable outcome of one of your efforts.

#168: Describe an ongoing problem you were able to overcome.

#169: Tell me about a project you completed ahead of schedule.

11. Career Aspirations

#170: Where do you hope that your career will have progressed to in the next few years?

#171: What are your long-term career plans?

#172: Since this will be your first job, how do you know you'll like the career path?

#173: Why is this job right for you at this time in your career?

#174: What are your aspirations beyond this job?

#175: What new challenges would you enjoy?

#176: If you could start all over again, what direction would your career take?

#177: What achievements have eluded you?

#178: How long do you think you'd continue to grow in this job?

#179: What career path interests you within the company?

#180: Compare this job to others you're pursuing.

#181: Have you progressed in your career as you expected?

#182: Tell me about your salary expectations.

#183: What do you reasonably expect to earn within five years?

#184: Have you ever taken a position that didn't fit into your long-term plan?

12. Personal Interests and Hobbies

#185: Other than work, tell me about an activity you've remained interested in over several years.

#186: What do you do in your spare time?

#187: Do you have a balanced lifestyle?

#188: What outside activities complement your work interests?

#189: Tell me about a time you were in a recreational setting and got an idea that helped in your work.

#190: How is your personality reflected in the kinds of activities you enjoy?

#191: What kinds of leisure activities help you perform your work better?

#192: What do you do to relax?

#193: If you found yourself getting burned out, what would you do to revitalize your energy?

#194: Our company believes that employees should give time back to the community. How do you feel about it?

#195: What community projects that can use your professional skills are particularly interesting to you?

#196: If you had unlimited leisure time, how would you spend that time?

#197: Describe how a sport or hobby taught you a lesson in teamwork or discipline.

#198: When you aren't at work, do you prefer to stick to a schedule, or do you prefer to be spontaneous? Why?

#199: Tell me about an interest that you outgrew.

#200: Describe a movie you've seen that really inspired you.

50 Zingers

#201: Tell me about a project in which you were disappointed with your personal performance.

#202: What would you do if I told you that I thought you were giving a very poor interview today?

#203: Tell me about your most difficult work or personal experience.

#204: If this were your first annual review with our company, what would I be telling you right now?

#205: Give an example of a time when you were asked to accomplish a task but weren't given enough information. How did you resolve this problem.

#206: Describe a time when you failed to resolve a conflict.

#207: How have you handled criticism of your work?

#208: What aspects of your work are most often criticized?

#209: Tell me about the last time you put your foot in your mouth.

#210: What might your current boss want to change about your work habits?

#211: Tell me about two or three aspects of your last job you'd never want to repeat.

#212: Tell me about a situation that frustrated you at work.

#213: Tell me about one of your projects that failed.

#214: Tell me about a time when your employer wasn't happy with your job performance.

#215: Have you ever been passed up for a promotion that you felt you deserved?

#216: Have you ever been fired?

#217: Why have you changed jobs so frequently?

#218: Why did you stay in your last job so long?

#219: Tell me about a problem you've had getting along with a work associate.

#220: Tell me about your least-favorite manager or professor.

#221: Who's the toughest employer you've ever had, and why?

#222: Have you ever had to work with a manager who was unfair to you, or who was just plain hard to get along with?

#223: Time management has become a necessary factor in productivity. Give an example of a time-management skill you've learned and applied at work.

#224: How do you handle tension with your boss?

#225: What would you say are the broad responsibilities of an editorial assistant?

#226: What is your current salary?

#227: Would you be willing to relocate to another city?

#228: Does the frequent travel required for this work fit into your lifestyle?

#229: Would you be able to work extended hours as necessary to perform the job?

#230: Sell me this stapler.

#231: How do you feel when things go wrong with a project? How do you handle it?

#232: Prove to me that your interest is sincere.

#233: Tell me about yourself.

#234: What is your biggest weakness?

#235: You have seven minutes to convince me why you're the best candidate for this position. Go.

#236: How would you respond to a defaulted form Z–65 counterderivative renewal request if your manager ordered you to do so, and if the policy under which the executive board resolves such issues were currently under review?

#237: Why weren't your grades better?

#238: Why did you decide to major in history?

#239: Was there a course that you found particularly challenging?

#240: Why didn't you participate more in extracurricular activities?

#241: Why do you want to leave your current position?

#242: Why would you want to leave an established career at an employment agency for an essentially entry-level position in marketing?

#243: Your resume doesn't list any job experience in the past few years. Why not?

#244: I see you've been out of work for a while. What difficulties have you had in finding a job that's compatible with your interests?

#245: Your resume indicates that you've been working for the past two years as a part-time clerk at Reliable Insurance Brokers. How will this experience help you in your banking career?

#246: What religion do you practice?

#247: How old are you?

#248: Are you married?

#249: Do you have children?

#250: Do you plan to have children?

INDEX